MW00668503

To my dear friends, the London family -

I hope that the ideas and themes in this book will add greater depth and meaning to your Passover seder and the story that stands at the foundation of our heritage. I have so much enjoyed our opportunities to study together and I hope we will have many more. I value our friendship tremendously! Thank you for your friendship and support!

Shlomo

THE FOUR ELEMENTS OF INNER FREEDOM

MOSAICA PRESS

The Exodus Story as a Model for Overcoming Challenges and Achieving Personal Breakthroughs

THE FOUR *elements* OF INNER FREEDOM

RABBI SHLOMO BUXBAUM

Author of The Four Elements of an Empowered Life

ISBN: 978-1-957579-64-1

Published by Mosaica Press, Inc.
www.mosaicapress.com
info@mosaicapress.com

ADVANCE PRAISE

RABBI JUDAH MISCHEL, AUTHOR OF BADERECH

In this next installment of his creative and insightful "Four Elements" series, Rabbi Shlomo Buxbaum has once again provided us with deep insight and tools for growth, and this time, has shown us the way toward unlocking the four elements of inner freedom. Rebbe Nachman of Breslov frames our redemption from *beis avadim*, the house of slavery, as an allusion to four categories of inner struggle, rooted in the four basic elements of creation. This beautiful new work unlocks ancient wisdom regarding one's personal life mission, providing practical, transformational guidance toward becoming truly free.

RABBI YAAKOV KLEIN, AUTHOR OF THE STORY OF OUR LIVES

The Four Elements of Inner Freedom by my dear friend Rabbi Shlomo Buxbaum is so much more than simply a book. In this genuine masterpiece, our hearts and minds are gifted a holistic system, an original path to help us accelerate our personal growth and spiritual development. Building upon his previous work on the four elements, Rabbi Shlomo Buxbaum brilliantly demonstrates the way these building blocks of Creation manifest throughout the Biblical narrative, a spiritual current underlying the epic adventure of human consciousness. As we delve deeply into the story of the Jewish nation's enslavement and eventual redemption from Egypt through the kaleidoscopic lens of R' Shlomo's system, we discover lessons bursting with illumination, warmth, clarity, relevance, and practical insight into our personal constrictions and how we, too, can achieve true inner freedom. I cannot recommend this book highly enough, and I think it will be of great value and benefit to whomever has the privilege of accepting its invitation to explore the Torah's inner light.

MENACHEM POZNANSKI, LCSW, AUTHOR OF **CONSCIOUSLY: SIX STEPS TO LIVING CONSCIOUSLY WITH OUR CREATOR**

Rabbi Shlomo Buxbaum does it again! In *The Four Elements of Inner Freedom*, Rabbi Buxbaum unpacks and teases out the practical yet ancient wisdom contained in the four elements of all reality, tackling themes and topics that are only becoming more and more relevant in our generation. Melding a grounded, almost scientific understanding of human behavior and habituation with a deeply spiritual message of hope, Rabbi Buxbaum delivers a true gem and gift for those seeking a spiritual life and a taste of inner freedom.

For my wife, Devorah

Your support, insight, and encouragement were the pillars upon which this book was created. May we merit to continue to share the beautiful *dvar Hashem* with our family, community, and the entire world.

For Meira, Shira Frayda, Moshe Mordechai, Simcha, Daniella Chava, and Asher

May you always be aware of Hashem's presence and guidance on every step of your journey. In times when you may feel stuck and in times when you may feel free, I daven that the lessons in this book will help you see the seas split before you.

This book is dedicated to our beloved grandparents,
the roots of our family tree. Each one of them in their
own way embodied the power of the human spirit
to overcome adversity, to build and to rebuild.

Rabbi Asher and Daniella Chaya Buxbaum, ob"m
R' Moshe Yehuda and Freeda Lowenstein, ob"m
R' Yissachar and Miryam Meyer, ob"m
Rabbi Simcha Moshe and Malka Wagner, ob"m

And in honor of

Rebbetzin Simmy Wagner

May Hashem grant her many more years
of good health and well-being.

With deep gratitude to all who supported this endeavor

Chaim and Miriam Buxbaum

Doniel and Suri Czermak

Nancee Gross and Mark Edelman

Zvi and Shoshana Gelt

Yitzchok Menachem and Gitty Haas

Erik and Connie Lindenauer

Avromi and Butchie Meyer

Rabbi Yaakov and Chaya Meyer

Dovi and Shoshana Ort

Avi and Suri Walles

Yossi and Ariella Zicherman

AYS Foundation
(In memory of Ari Yeruchem Ben Dovid Zalman Halevi, ob"m)

מוסדות אור שמח מרכז טננבאום ע.ר. 58-00-21343-00
רח' שמעון הצדיק 22-28 ירושלים ת.ד. 18103
טל: 02-581-0315

Michtav Bracha

Av 5782

"Each person must regard themselves as if they were liberated from Mitzraim." Mitzraim is not only a country, and *Yetzias Mitzraim* is not only a historical event. Mitzraim represents all of the constrictions, limitations, and inhibitions that enslave us from within and prevent us from attaining our potential and becoming the person we were destined to be. And the failure to become that person is the ultimate source of unhappiness, frustration, and despair. *Yetzias Mitzraim* is the journey of leaving those constraints and boundaries, discovering purpose, vibrancy, joy, and *kirvas Elokim* (closeness to God). But many of us lack the tools to undertake this journey. We either lack a sense of direction or are so enmeshed in our personal slavery that we lack the desire to begin the trip or feel unable to do so.

Rabbi Shlomo Buxbaum offers us a map through this terrain, coupling it with the necessary supplies. He has written a truly extraordinary, indeed breathtaking book, outlining the steps we can take in the personal journey from inner slavery to freedom. Solidly based on Torah sources and augmented by profound psychological insight, this work is chockfull of beautiful thoughts, coupled with very practical suggestions. This book will teach all of us how to make our lives better, how to fill our days with meaning, how to integrate our mind with our heart, how to be a Jew, how to be a human being, and how to feel the loving embrace of our Creator.

We owe the author a great debt of gratitude for enabling and empowering us *b'chasdei Hashem* to achieve our own personal *Yetzias Mitzraim*.

Yitzchak A. Breitowitz
Rav, Kehillat Ohr Somayach
Jerusalem, Israel

Our holy Sages teach that our human flaws are compared to the four elements: earth, water, wind and fire. Every single one of us will struggle in our lifetime with these four elements in our own personal way. The Chasidic masters, Rebbe Nachman of Breslov among them, saw hints to that inner struggle in the story of the Jewish people being enslaved in Egypt and ultimately being freed.

In this wonderful work, the author, Rabbi Shlomo Buxbaum, explores this connection in depth, as he weaves together ideas from a variety of sifrei mussar, machshava, and chassidus to take us on our own journey our of our personal Mitzrayim. This work is filled with deep wisdom, powerful lessons, and practical life advice, presented in a way that is clear to the reader and immediately applicable to one's life.

Rabbi Buxbaum has been a member of the Breslov Torah chaburah for several years and is one who seeks to deeply understand the inner works of chassidus and pnimiyus haTorah. I wish him much success in the publishing of this work and blessings to all of the readers who are going on this journey with him.

May Hashem give all of us the strength to become masters of our inner nature and overcome all of our personal struggles!

Nasan Maimon

R' Nasan Maimon

רח' הרב סלנט 36 מאה שערים 36 Harav Salant st. Meah Shearim | טל. Tel. 02-6273067 | ת.ד. P.O.B. 5023 | נוסד תר"פ | ע.ר. 58-011-890-9

The following approbation was written for the author's previous book, The Four Elements of an Empowered Life.

תפארת גדליה

YGW

בס"ד

From the Desk of

RABBI AHRON LOPIANSKY

Rosh HaYeshiva

Chanukah 5780

In a society filled with well-intentioned people who are scheming how to "fix the world," Rabbi Shlomo Buxbaum reminds us most powerfully that we first have to fix ourselves. Not only is this a prerequisite for healing the world but actually is the very beginning of that process. Rabbi Buxbaum uses authentic and ancient Jewish sources, drawing much on mysticism, and succeeds in translating it to a language and ideas that are accessible to the modern student.

This book is meant for the person who can seriously introspect, understand the multifaceted nature of the human, and how Torah addresses all of these various facets. It is sure to add much depth and comprehension to that person. Hopefully, we will succeed in fixing ourselves first — one facet at a time, and the world — one human being at a time!

Ahron Shraga Lopiansky

YESHIVA OF GREATER WASHINGTON – TIFERES GEDALIAH

1216 ARCOLA AVENUE, SILVER SPRING, MD 20902 ▪ 301-649-7077 ▪ WWW.YESHIVA.EDU

TABLE OF CONTENTS

ACKNOWLEDGMENTS

LIFE IS A GREAT ADVENTURE that parallels the story of the Exodus.

Our soul descends into this constricted world, just like the Israelites' descent into Egypt. We fall, we struggle, and, hopefully, we rise up and emerge victorious. Maybe we'll notice all the little miracles happening in the backdrop. And if we follow in our ancestors' footsteps, we will manifest freedom in the deepest possible way. Along the way, we will make discoveries about ourselves, about God, and about the people around us.

The Book of Exodus begins with the story of a nation, but it then becomes the story of heroic individuals—Moses, Aaron, Miriam, and other good guys and bad guys that we meet along the journey. Our own personal journey too is not a solo expedition. It is about the fascinating individuals who join us on the journey. Some of those individuals will be there from start to finish, others will join us when the time is right, and some will just pop in and out. But if we keep in mind that everyone in our life is God-sent to impact our life in some way or another, we really start to take notice of the people around us in a much deeper way. We value their involvement and learn to be so much more grateful.

This book is about living that journey. It is about seeing the Exodus story unfold in our daily life. And, therefore, what better way to open the book than to acknowledge many of the heroes in my journey, the ones who have both laid the foundation for me in my life and my career, and those who have helped to make this book a reality.

The Exodus story is first and foremost about having gratitude to the Almighty for taking a nation that didn't actually deserve to be redeemed and raising them up to the greatest heights. On a personal note, I feel that I have been able to see the loving *yad Hashem* in my life, and I am so grateful and humbled for that.

My parents, R' Chaim and Miriam Buxbaum, and my in-laws, Rabbi Yaakov and Chaya Meyer, continue to be that foundation in every way possible. My siblings and siblings-in-law are an endless source of support and inspiration.

I have the great privilege of directing a wonderful organization called The Lev Experience, which awards me the opportunity to meet and teach Torah to Jews of all backgrounds. So much of this book is an outgrowth of the classes, learning, and coaching that have happened under that umbrella. It has also been the platform from which I am able to pursue my creative ambitions and create content, such as this book, to reach an even wider audience. Thank you to my wonderful partners and supporters in building The Lev Experience for your excitement and encouragement about all of our projects, and especially this one.

I also have the privilege to be a part of the Rabbinic staff of Mesorah DC, led by Rabbi Zvi Teitelbaum. Thank you to the entire Mesorah family, who have opened your hearts to learn from me, to share your lives with me, and for all your enthusiasm for these projects.

As you will read in the introduction, the concept of this book came as I was learning *Likutei Moharan* with my *chavrusa*, Chaim Spillman. Chaim also introduced me to Rabbi Nasan Maimon, who has been a wellspring of wisdom and inspiration for me over the past two years. Yossi Lanton has also been a tremendous part in helping me forge and further my relationship with Rav Nasan.

I am deeply indebted to the yeshivos that formed the foundation of my learning: Toras Moshe, Mir, Aish HaTorah, and the shuls and Torah institutions of Silver Spring, MD, which support me in my ongoing effort to grow spiritually and to raise a family in the path of Torah and mitzvos. I am indebted to all of the local rabbonim and *talmidei chachamim*, and consider myself unbelievably fortunate to be in a community that is led by the great Rav Ahron Lopiansky.

The book is a continuation of a journey that began with the writing of my first book, *The Four Elements of an Empowered Life*. The wide reach and success of that book was very much due to my friends and colleagues who supported me by starting book clubs, bringing me to their communities to speak, and sharing the book with others. The list is too long to mention, but please know that I really appreciate you.

Thank you to Rabbi Yitzchak Breitowitz, and my dear friends Menachem Poznanski, Rabbi Judah Mischel, and Rabbi Yaakov Klein for looking over the manuscript, for all of your encouragement, and for writing approbations for this book. Thank you to the amazing family and friends who financially supported this project. It could not have happened without you.

The staff of Mosaica Press are the best in the business. Thank you, Rabbi Yaacov Haber, Rabbi Doron Kornbluth, Robert Sussman, my dear friend Shui Haber, and all of the staff for running a world-class operation and making me feel so valued as an author.

Lastly, to my very special family. To my wife, Devorah, who thoroughly reviewed every word of the original draft and helped craft it into a piece of literature that would be relatable and have wide appeal. Thank you for being my partner in life and in work, and for tolerating my disappearing for hours at a time to work on this book. Thank you for your encouragement and excitement about this project and all of our projects together. And to my six beautiful children, thank you guys for rooting for me and for being such a crucial part of our mission!

While I have done my absolute best to offer an approach that is based on authentic Torah sources, it should be noted that while quoting sources out of their original context, I might have inadvertently misrepresented what the original authors' true intentions were. If that is the case, I accept full responsibility and hope that any misinformation should not reflect negatively on any of the works quoted.

The teachings and ideas that are contained in this work are ones that have personally impacted my life and have shaped the way I approach the world. I hope that I have done justice to deliver it to you in the clearest possible way. I pray that you, my friends, the readers, will find in this book clarity, hope, and inspiration on your own journey toward your own personal "promised land."

I welcome any feedback and comments and certainly any success stories that may result from reading this book. I can be reached at my email, shlomo@levx.org.

INTRODUCTION

"The Exodus from Mitzrayim occurs in every human being, in every era, in every year, and even on every day."

Rabbi Natan of Breslov, quoting Rabbi Nachman of Breslov

IN THE LATE 1990S, a social psychologist by the name of Roy Baumeister and several of his colleagues proposed a concept known as *ego depletion*, or what would become more widely known as *decision fatigue*. They suggested that human beings have a limited mental capacity to exercise their willpower, use self-control, and make decisions. The more decisions that a person must make, the more his mental resources are drained, making it harder and harder to make good decisions and overcome temptations. Experiments showed that a person who had to resist eating chocolate was less likely to be successful at completing a complex puzzle and vice versa.

Put differently, we can say that the more choices one has, the more those choices may be enslaving the person in the long term. This is very important for you and me to consider, as we have been privileged to be born into a life of choices, the likes of which history has never seen.

Think about all the decisions that you have already made today. Did you make it an early morning, or did you treat yourself to a few extra hits of the snooze button? How many possible outfits did you have to sort through before you decided what to wear? Did you begin your day by going straight to your tasks, or did you take some time for your own self-care? And, if a coffee was your morning beverage of choice, did you go for instant or brewed, caffeinated or decaf, sweetened or unsweetened, large or small, grande or venti, light or black, or countless other variations?

And all these choices were just the start of a day in which you went about engaging in a life that you most likely constructed based on your own preferences and desires. According to the theory of decision fatigue, the ability to make all these choices may be hurting us in the long run, hampering our ability to focus on the real puzzles of life and make good decisions regarding the things that really matter. All the decisions and options may be depleting us from being able to really look at the most important aspects of our life and making the choices that will truly help us live a life of greatness!

Decision fatigue is just one example of how the outer optics of freedom and choice doesn't always mean that we are truly free. Sure, we are free from oppressive masters abusing us and robbing us of our rights. But does that mean that we have no masters controlling us? Is it possible that the alarm clock and the coffee, the thirty-two flavors of ice cream, and the Star-Spangled Banner are all creating this big illusion orchestrated to make us feel free, while distracting us from the true, inner experience of freedom? Can it be that we are externally free but internally trapped—and we don't even realize it?

The world of fantasy, fiction, and fairy tale has told many tales of characters placed in a world that was completely manufactured—a dystopian society, a big computer program, a movie set, or a video game, perhaps—in order to breed some sort of ignorance or obedience. We may see the protagonist of such a story at first going about his daily life in this perfectly curated environment, unaware that the reality he is experiencing is purely artificial. Some manipulative intelligence is behind it all with some agenda. He is like a child born as a prisoner but never told that there is something wrong with his current situation.

But then something goes wrong. There is a glitch in the system—an informer, or just an inner sense that something isn't right. The hero takes notice of some small subtle aspects of his life that seem off, creating an inner feeling of discomfort, an inner voice that yearns for something more. This sparks a deep search and ultimately an exciting adventure, a quest to discover true freedom. Even though this plastic world that he is in may be more pleasant than the frightening reality on the other side, still we root for our hero to beat the bad guys and slay the dragons that are discovered along the way. This is because we deeply believe, no matter what, that true freedom is the ultimate destination.

When we look closely at our own life, we need to ask ourselves: Are we like the protagonist in that story, walking around with an assumption that we are free because there is no forceful entity standing over us, unaware that we may lack the truest type of freedom? Are we complacent in the simulation, or do we have the wherewithal to push back and start searching for something bigger? Are we OK with just being OK?

WHAT IS INNER FREEDOM?

Inner freedom is a concept that has emerged in the world of personal development and positive psychology as the desired destination for anyone truly looking to live life to the fullest. It is born out of the awareness that most of what holds us back from reaching our dreams is actually ourselves: Our own mindsets and limiting beliefs. Our own habits and lack of motivation. Our own fears and anxiety. Our own resistance and excuses. Our own lack of clarity and belief in ourselves. Our own weaknesses and ego. Inner freedom is the ability to identify and overcome the inner forces that try to distract and derail us from living as our greatest possible selves.

Most of us are trying to juggle a lot. There are the expectations, the responsibilities, and the needs of our day-to-day life. Just getting through the day trying to navigate all those things consumes our focus and our energy. The amount of effort it takes just to maintain the status quo of our life is tremendous. And because of the Herculean effort to just get through it all, we stop dreaming. We lose focus of the bigger picture, or maybe we never had it in the first place.

All this turmoil is the norm in the life of any growth-oriented person. It is natural, and it is good. But one must wonder: Is this freedom? If we are on a road that won't lead to the greatest version of ourselves, are we just experiencing a different form of slavery?

Inner freedom is not about throwing off the yoke of our day-to-day responsibilities, living life not caring what other people have to say, or becoming a rebel against society. What it does mean is this:

- Seeing our life as one of endless potential, rather than feeling trapped in our current situation
- Making decisions from a place of clarity, courage, and abundance, rather than pressure, fear, or pre-conditioning
- Living in a way that we not only *believe* in, but *feel* inspired and excited by
- Expressing ourselves freely without insecurity or fear of judgment from others
- Fully accepting ourselves—both our strengths and weaknesses—without constant feelings of insecurity and inconsistency

Inner freedom is, perhaps, the foundation that all true happiness is built upon, and even is the definition of happiness itself! We can go so far as to say that the entire purpose of our life is to achieve true inner freedom. No one is born with it. It isn't something that comes naturally. It is the one constant that we can say every human being walking the planet is working on. That means that if we are to truly live a life of happiness and purpose, we are going to have to develop the tools to access our inner freedom.

INNER FREEDOM IS, PERHAPS, THE FOUNDATION THAT ALL TRUE HAPPINESS IS BUILT UPON.

If we understand the beautiful wisdom of our Jewish tradition, we can see that we actually have all the wisdom and the tools necessary to achieve such freedom. We can follow an ancient yet timeless plan that will take us step-by-step through the process needed to break through those personal entrapments and all those internal masters, and truly experience the freedom for which we are so badly yearning!

And what better place in Torah to look for guidance on how to live a life of freedom than the greatest story of liberation that humanity has ever known: The Book of *Shemos* (Exodus), the story of the Jewish People leaving Egypt. On the surface, the story of the Exodus may seem to be a piece of history, a tale of physical oppression, great miracles, and the beginnings of the story of our nationhood. But looking at it in this way might distract us from what is a gold mine of the most important practical life lessons for us on how to live with true freedom.

The Torah is Judaism's ultimate guidebook for living life to its maximum potential. All of the brilliant ideas that have ever moved humanity are in it. And the story of the Exodus is the blueprint for anyone who feels trapped in any way in his life to discover a path toward breakthrough, recovery, and healing.

And while there are a plethora of books, essays, and articles that explore the Exodus and bring out those lessons, I believe that this book has something very unique to offer.

WHY I WROTE THIS BOOK

The journey to inner freedom is a process of deep introspection and self-awareness. It is about understanding ourselves and why we act the way we do. One who does not know the ins and outs of his inner world cannot possibly take the steps necessary to leave their personal Egypt and become the greatest possible version of himself.

In June 2021, I experienced the great blessing of releasing my first book, *The Four Elements of an Empowered Life: A Guidebook to Discovering Your Inner World and Unique Purpose*. The book was based on a powerful idea that is part of ancient Jewish wisdom and spoken about throughout the ages by our sages, Torah scholars, and Kabbalists. The basic premise is that just as all matter can be categorized as earth, water, wind, or fire (i.e., solid, liquid, gas, or pure energy/plasma), so too, our inner world—the world of our consciousness, our thoughts, our emotions, etc.—is a reflection of those elements. This means that there is a part of our personality that is like each of these things: earth, water, wind, and fire.

The book was a journey into the world of the elements, showing how through mastery of the struggles that exists within each of these realms, we can reach self-mastery and discover the unique purpose for which we were put on this world. It was also a deep dive into the Book of *Bereishis* (Genesis), which is the foundation of all of Torah and all of Judaism, showing how the early generations of mankind specifically struggled and corrupted themselves in the arena of the four elements. The patriarchs and matriarchs came along and, through their struggles, perfected themselves in these areas and restored the holiness to the four elements.

In the months after the book's release, many readers shared with me how deeply these ideas resonated with them and how these ancient teachings guided them to making personal breakthroughs in their own struggle. Furthermore, many readers felt that it gave them a fresh perspective on the lives of our ancestors to whom they had previously felt completely disconnected.

Just as I began to contemplate whether there was room in the wellsprings of Jewish literature for another commentary on the Book the Exodus, I came across a very powerful statement from the great Chassidic master and mystic, Rabbi Nachman of Breslov. Commenting on the very first verse in the Ten Commandments, "I am God who took you out of the house of slavery," which is referring to Egypt, Rabbi Nachman explains that "the house of slavery alludes to the four inner struggles that are connected to the four elements."

As I began to explore this profound and eye-opening connection between the Exodus and the four elements, I discovered beautiful gems and life-changing ideas at every corner. Not only did this story that I grew up with and studied all my life take on a whole new meaning, but I saw new angles and depth in the ideas and principles that I had written about in my first book. The connections between the book of *Bereishis* and *Shemos* began to leap off the page and click together like a puzzle in a way that I had never before understood.

The focus of this book is different from *The Four Elements of an Empowered Life*. There, we focused on the tools and habits to discover our mission. Here, we focus on the tools and strategies to break free from the mindsets and pursuits that may be holding us back from accomplishing our mission, or as we refer to it in the book, "the inner Pharaoh."

For those who read the first book, you will find this work to be a beautiful structure built on its foundation. For those who did not yet read the first book, fear not! The points that are necessary for this work are included here as well. My hope is that the incredible value that you find in these pages will inspire you to go back and read the first book as well.

My greatest wish, though, is that this will be more than just a "read." It will be the beginning of a journey for you, wherever you may find yourself, to move beyond your self-imposed constraints and discover the inner freedom for which you are searching!

From The Four Elements of an Empowered Life:

WE EXIST IN BOTH an external world and an internal world. Our external world is filled with the people with whom we interact, the places where we go, and the environment that surrounds us. Our internal world is the world of our consciousness. Look deeply inward, and you will find a fascinating and complex inner world.

Kabbalah (and many other ancient philosophies) spoke of the four fundamental elements of creation: fire, wind, water, and earth. These four elements reflect the four states that all matter exists in: Plasma, Gas, Liquid, and Solid.

Everything that exists in the external world on a macro level is reflected on a micro level inside us, having some expression and manifestation in our inner world. Therefore, when exploring the inner world of man, the various different domains that make up the *nefesh* can be said to follow the very same pattern of fire, wind, water, and earth:

- Earth—the domain of physicality
- Water—the domain of the emotions and desires
- Wind—the domain of the intellect and communication
- Fire—the domain of the will and the ego

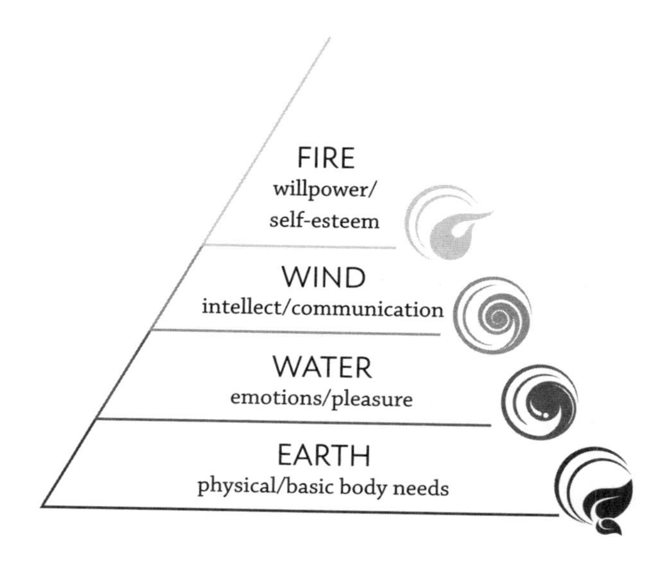

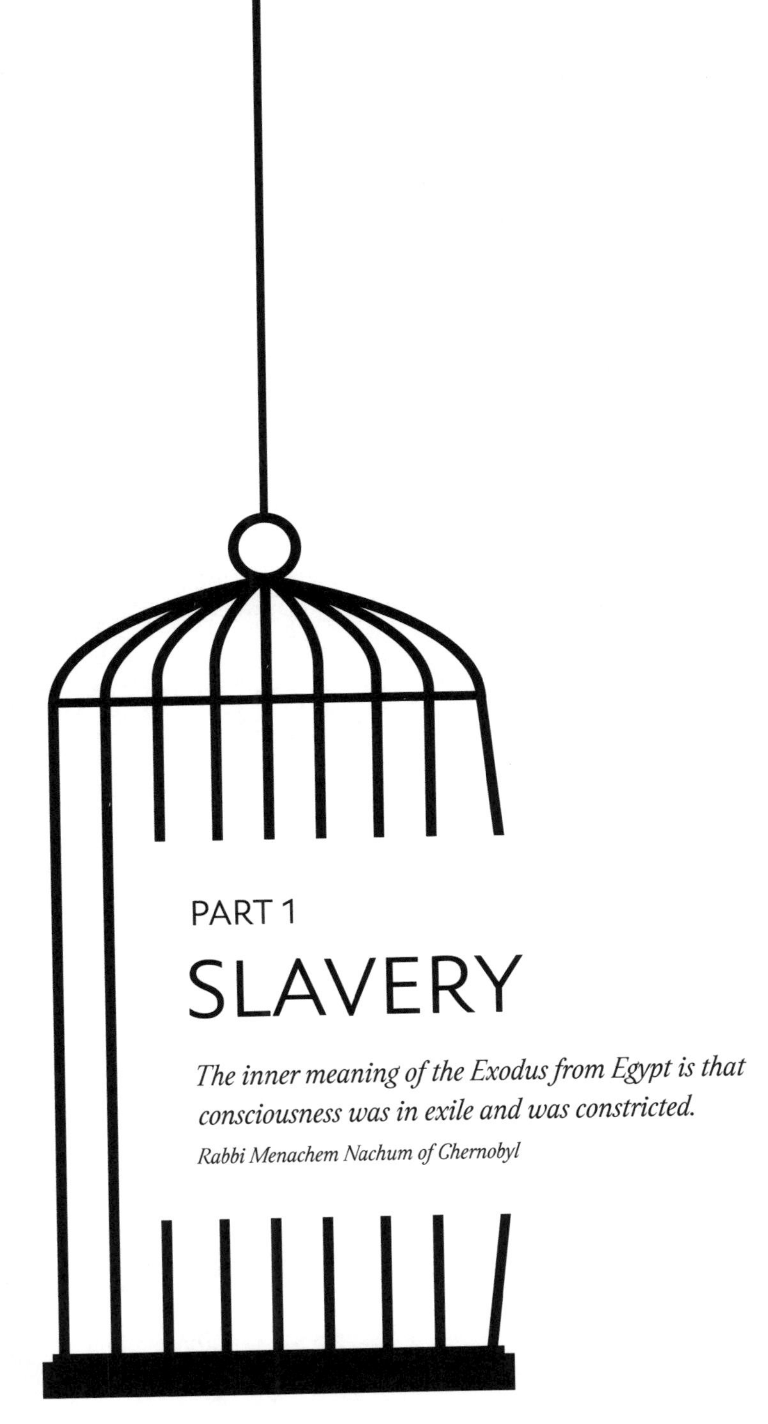

PART 1

SLAVERY

The inner meaning of the Exodus from Egypt is that consciousness was in exile and was constricted.

Rabbi Menachem Nachum of Chernobyl

chapter one

WHY WE STRUGGLE

FREEDOM

Freedom is one of the most prized possessions of the modern world. We will protect it at all costs and wage great battles to defend it. The flourishing of human rights and liberties over the better part of the last two centuries is one of the great modern achievements of the Western world, as we have embraced the idea that "all human beings are born free and equal in dignity and rights."[1]

Freedom takes a prominent place in Jewish tradition as well. The Jewish People were born out of a process of enslavement and freedom, directly experiencing what is arguably the greatest liberation story the world has ever known.

We were slaves to Pharaoh in Egypt, and God took us out from there with a strong hand and an outstretched arm...

These words, familiar to many Jews from the Passover Seder, are the words that the author of the Haggadah uses to open the discussion about the most significant story in the history of mankind, and the centerpiece of the Jewish story.

Close to three thousand years ago, the Israelites descended from the land of Canaan to the land of Egypt because of a famine in the land. They began as a family of only seventy people, but before long grew to become a large nation. Though this immigrant nation was obedient to the laws of the land and contributed greatly to its infrastructure, the proliferation of this foreign group of people with their own dress and their own language worried the Egyptians greatly. What began as royal

---

1 Universal Declaration of Human Rights.

treatment turned into oppressive slavery that would last for close to a century of their 210-year stay.

At the point that the oppression was no longer tolerable, God heard their cries and intervened by sending Moses, a righteous and humble leader armed with ten powerful plagues to rain down upon Egypt. Eventually, Pharaoh expelled the Jewish People from Egypt, only to have a change of heart less than a week later. The Egyptians chased after the liberated nation, only to be decimated at the Sea of Reeds in the greatest display of miraculous events that humankind has ever seen. God then raised the nation to spiritual greatness by giving them the Torah at Mount Sinai and bestowing upon them the status of a "kingdom of priests and a holy nation."

This incredible story stands at the core of Jewish life and shapes so much of Jewish practice. It is the foundation of our faith and the symbol of our closeness to God. "I am the Lord your God who has taken you out of Egypt" is God's way of introducing himself to the Jewish People for the very first time when they stood at the foot of Mount Sinai. Of all the ways that God could be introduced—Creator, Sustainer, Father, King, etc.—all of those roles seem to be captured in that one expression.

We mention the Exodus story several times a day in our services and meal blessings. It is a central focus in the special *Kiddush* blessings that we recite on Shabbat and on Jewish holidays, and, of course, the holiday of Passover is completely dedicated to the Exodus story.

One has to wonder, however, why this story is such a major focus of Jewish life. While it is certainly necessary to know your beginnings and to infuse a heritage with the values that are at its roots, that still doesn't quite explain why the story itself needs to be on our minds seemingly all the time!

The answer is that the Exodus story is meant to be much more than a historical event or a tale about the beginnings of the Jewish nation. Jewish wisdom sees all the Torah stories as more than just historical events. Such stories set the precedent for what happens to every individual in some way in his own life. When viewed through these glasses, the Torah comes alive and becomes a guidebook for how to live a life of greatness. This is true with all the stories, and the story of the Exodus is certainly no exception.

MITZRAYIM

The Hebrew word for Egypt, *Mitzrayim*, comes from the word *meitzar*, meaning constriction or narrowness. When we speak of Mitzrayim, we are not only speaking about a geographical location, but also a state of entrapment in a place of constriction in one's life. It is an ongoing story of struggle and redemption that happens in our lives on so many levels as we try to discover true freedom.

The freedom that we refer to here is not physical freedom, political freedom, or religious freedom, but something much deeper. There are many forms of enslavement—some obvious and some subtle, some external and some internal. Mitzrayim is symbolic of those times in our life when we feel trapped in situations that seem beyond our control. It is symbolic of times when we feel enslaved by others or even by our own selves.

As we learn about this enslavement, our task is to look inward and determine the particular form of enslavement that is relevant to our lives. Leaving Mitzrayim, then, is symbolic of our own breakthrough from those narrow confines to achieve the ultimate freedom for which we so badly yearn.

In many ways, we can view our entire life as a journey from the confines of Egypt on a quest to discover our own "promised land." Every single human being is placed in this world with his own set of struggles. It may be the narrow and limiting beliefs that we picked up in the early years of our life or a bad habit/addiction that makes us feel powerless. It may be a toxic life situation in which we are stuck with no clear way out, or a spiritual rut, feeling that we are drifting further and further away.

And, perhaps, we have grown completely numb to our enslavement and have learned to accept things the way that they are. This, too, is a form of slavery. As the old Chassidic saying goes, "The real exile of Israel in Egypt was that they learned to endure it."

The Exodus story as a paradigm for our personal liberation is meant to provide us with more than just an inspirational boost or a pep talk to never give up hope. We are meant to see it as a guide that maps out the step-by-step journey we all must take in our own quest for liberation. The more that we delve into the depth and details of the story, the more we can extract the lessons, the tools, and the mindsets that we can apply to our life. The story of the Exodus teaches us how to identify the major obstacles and barriers in life and overcome them. This happens when we combine courage with faith and when we take concrete actions forward while allowing the hand of Divine providence guide us along our journey.

THE STORY OF THE EXODUS TEACHES US HOW TO IDENTIFY THE MAJOR OBSTACLES AND BARRIERS IN LIFE AND OVERCOME THEM.

SUFFERING AND OUR MISSION

A core Jewish belief is that everything happens for a purpose and is part of a master plan. The Torah commentators, therefore, wonder why it was necessary for the Jewish nation to be enslaved in Egypt in the first place. Why was this part of God's master plan for them?

Similar questions tug at the heart of anyone going through a dark time in his life: Why is this happening? Why is this happening *to me*? You have probably wondered at some point in your life, as I have: Why do I seem to have it harder than others?

What makes the Egyptian exile so much more puzzling is that God actually informed Abraham many years earlier—before he even had any children!—that his descendants would be exiled in a foreign land for four hundred years. Abraham, who reached out to and defended all sorts of wicked people, including the evil people of Sodom, accepts this information without even putting up any sort of argument! Why wouldn't Abraham try to argue on behalf of his grandchildren, his own flesh and blood, at least the same way that he defended Sodom?

The answer to these questions is that the enslavement in Egypt was all part of a process, a prerequisite for the Jewish People to eventually stand at Mount Sinai and receive the Torah. The master plan, which Abraham understood, was that Egypt would act as an incubator for the Jewish People to refine their character by becoming detached from the material world and achieving mastery over their inner flaws.

The same is true with our personal struggles. Every single person is given a specific set of struggles that is connected to his own mission and process of refinement. Your challenges are very specific to you, just as mine are to me. Nothing is random. But how God pairs a specific challenge or set of challenges with a specific person is far beyond our understanding. There is something rooted deep down in our soul, some light that needs to be awakened and brought out of us, that only God sees and understands.

But as far as we are concerned, our life provides us with constant opportunities through our struggles to develop our character and our inner world. The more that we learn how to navigate life's challenges in every area of our life, the more we are refining our character and our soul in the process.

The Jewish People's enslavement in the land of Egypt was no coincidence at all. The fact that God put them in the most corrupt land where they would have to undergo not only physical slavery but immersion in the culture of the most immoral of lands, to such an extent that they themselves nearly sank to the lowest depth of impurity, was all very specific and part of God's master plan. Eventually, they would emerge and rebuild even stronger, refining their character at its core and reaching even greater heights than they could have prior to their enslavement.

The great Torah commentators compare the Jewish People's enslavement in Egypt, and the personal Egypt that we all encounter, to the process of refining gold.[2] Gold does not naturally exist in its purest form. After it is extracted from the minerals, rocks, and mud in the earth, it is mixed with many impurities that need to be removed through an intense refinement process. That process involves taking the gold, placing it in a furnace that has been heated up to an incredibly high temperature, and melting it down. This causes the impurities and other foreign substances to separate, and the pure gold can then be extracted with all the other impurities left behind.

---

2 *Alshich, Parashas Shemos.*

The Israelites, the children of the holy patriarchs and matriarchs, were like gold mixed with all sorts of impurities from the early sins of humanity. For the first two thousand years of the history of mankind, man had become completely steeped in a sinful way of life; the impurity of sin had become part and parcel of the DNA of human beings. One needs to simply refer back to the early stories of the Torah, starting from when Adam and Eve were evicted from the Garden of Eden, to see the extent of the early corruption:

- Cain and Abel, the first human children, get into a terrible fight that results in a disgruntled and depressed Cain murdering his brother, the very first depression-driven homicide in human history.
- Humanity falls deeper and deeper into paganism and sexual immorality until God decides to destroy the world with a massive flood, saving only the righteous Noah and his family.
- The world rebuilds only to unite together and try to wage war against God by building the infamous Tower of Bavel.
- Finally, the righteous Abraham comes onto the scene and tries to teach faith and kindness to the world, in contrast to the powerful and evil city of Sodom that has become the world capital of narcissism and corruption.

It was against this backdrop that the foundation for the Jewish People was set, with their eventual mission to be a light unto the world. There is no way that any nation could have been on a level to receive such an exalted mission and prophecy unless they underwent some sort of deep refining process.

That refinement process began with the adventures of the patriarchs Abraham, Isaac, and Jacob, and the matriarchs Sarah, Rebecca, Rachel, and Leah. It then came to full fruition with the birth of their descendants in the fiery furnace of the Egyptian exile.

Egypt, the world power of the time, was like the furnace that caused the Jewish People to melt down and extract their essence from the impure shell—not only through physical oppression, but by their spiritual influence on them. The Jewish People sinking to the lowest levels of impurities was like seeing the impurities of gold separate. True, the impurities become much more obvious and noticeable, but it also allows the pure gold to be easily extracted.

We can understand, therefore, why the Egyptian exile was indeed necessary for the Jewish People, and why it was destined to happen already many years earlier when God told Abraham, "Your children will be in exile for four hundred years."[3]

In our own lives as well, we are on a journey of refinement. We are like that precious piece of gold with a soul that radiates with beauty. But it isn't yet in its purest form. It has all sorts of impurities that attached to it for reasons beyond our understanding. Life will provide the necessary heat to bring all of that up to the surface and give us an opportunity to refine it. And when we do, we become even greater than had we never had to struggle with it in the first place.

WE ARE LIKE THAT PRECIOUS PIECE OF GOLD WITH A SOUL THAT RADIATES WITH BEAUTY. BUT IT ISN'T YET IN ITS PUREST FORM.

This can be understood better by comparing two people, both of whom are trying to refrain from a specific behavior. One of them is aware of the danger of the bad behavior but never experienced it or witnessed it firsthand. Though intellectually he knows that it is problematic, there may still be an aspect of curiosity or some temptation to taste what is forbidden. And if nothing else, he wonders whether he would be strong enough to resist the temptation if it would arise.

The other has fallen prey in the past, or has seen others, and has a much deeper awareness, not only the negative consequences, but also the pain, guilt, and shame that follows. This experiential knowledge of the outcome has created a revulsion to it. Even if the temptation does arise from time to time, it is countered by an equally powerful voice reminding him of the other perspective. And even if he is overcome by the temptation, he can't fully enjoy it because he is aware of the consequences that will follow.

---

3 The number 400 is a multiple of forty. In Kabbalistic numerology, forty is considered a number of refinement and rebirth.

We would surely say that the second fellow has achieved an even higher and deeper self-mastery than the first. This deep refinement is, in fact, the life mission of so many people, especially those who seem to find themselves constantly staring down the barrel of unhealthy habits, addictions, and personal struggles in their life.

Therefore, the more we learn about our inner world that we are here to refine, the more we will be able to understand the purpose of our challenges and how to navigate through them using the power and the tools innately part of our personality.

As we will see in the upcoming chapters, Egypt was exactly what the Jewish People needed to reach their exalted level. Every challenge that Egypt presented was directly connected to a muscle that the Jewish People needed to develop. Our challenges are also exactly what we need to accomplish our mission, and the more we learn to see that, we become rulers over those challenges, rather than allowing them to rule over us.

The word RULE is a great acronym for the steps necessary to achieve. It stands for Recognize, Understand, Learn, and Elevate. Our journey to self-mastery requires us to do the following:

- RECOGNIZE the specific challenges that keep coming our way.
- UNDERSTAND their purpose by identifying where inside us the challenge is coming from and what inner muscle it is meant to developed. We then need to...
- LEARN from our experiences and our ancient wisdom the tools and strategies necessary to developing those muscles, until we are able to...
- ELEVATE those parts of ourselves, so that instead of the challenges bringing us down, we see them as a tool for growth and elevation. This will all become clear as our journey unfolds.

In the upcoming chapters, we will learn how to RULE over our inner world. We will come to recognize the different elements that are the foundations of our personalities and understand ourselves in the deepest possible way. We will learn the tools necessary to activate the most positive aspects of ourselves and how we can elevate ourselves to become the greatest that we can be.

summary

- The Exodus story is meant to set the precedent for our own lives. The Hebrew word for Egypt, *Mitzrayim*, comes from the word *meitzar*, meaning constriction or narrowness, representing a state of entrapment in a place of constriction in one's life.
- The enslavement in Egypt was part of a process to refine the Jewish nation from all sorts of impurities caused by the grave sins of the first two thousand years of humanity that had become part and parcel of humanity's DNA. It was a prerequisite for the Jewish People to eventually stand at Mount Sinai and receive the Torah.
- Every individual is on a personal journey of refinement. We are each given a specific set of struggles that is connected to our own personal mission to refine ourselves and awaken our souls. When we learn how to RULE (Recognize, Understand, Learn from, and Elevate) over our challenges, we become greater than had we not faced the challenge in the first place.

chapter two

THE FOUR CUPS AND THE FOUR ELEMENTS

THE FOUR CUPS OF FREEDOM

The Passover Seder is a sacred tradition that is a pillar of Jewish life for Jews of all backgrounds. Each year, going back thousands of years, Jews around the world get together with family and friends on the evening of the fifteenth of Nissan to celebrate the anniversary and tell over the story of the birth of the Jewish People—about the enslavement in Egypt and the miraculous liberation that happened on that night. It's a highlight of the year for many adults and children alike, and is a formative moment in the development of one's Jewish identity.

Like many aspects of Judaism, the customs and the general feel of the Seder vary widely from family to family—different tunes, different props, and, of course, countless recipes for the traditional Passover dishes. In some homes, the Passover Seder is of a more serious feel and in others it is more fun; some kid-friendly and some adults-only; some more spiritual and some more social. But there are some things, like matzoh and maror, which are essential to making it a Seder. The four cups of wine that are strategically drunk at different points of the Seder are one of those essential features.

Interestingly, the cups are not the only time that the number four is present at the Seder. The Seder is actually filled with "fours," such as the "four questions" of the *Mah Nishtanah* and the questions of the four categories of children: the wise one, the wicked one, the simple one, and the one who doesn't know to ask.

What is all of this emphasis on the number four?

Our Sages point to the fact that when God was informing Moses of the imminent redemption of the Jewish People from Egypt, He used four terms of redemption:

- *Ve'hotzeisi*—I will take you out from under the burdens of Egypt.
- *Ve'hitzalti*—I will save you from their servitude.
- *Ve'gaalti*—I will redeem you.
- *Ve'lakachti*—I will take you to be My people.

These four powerful phrases, *the four promises of redemption*, carry with them powerful ramifications for all of history, and for you and me, as they contain within them the entire secret of exile and redemption. If we understand the secret to these words, we can see that they are a roadmap for us and for our own personal journey. They contain the secret to achieving self-mastery, to refining our inner diamond, and to revealing our soul.

THE FOUR ELEMENTS

We are all aware that man is a combination of a physical body and a spiritual soul. But, in fact, we are much more complex than that. In between these two extremes of the body, which is the vehicle, and the soul, which is a Divine spark of Godliness, is a fascinating and complex inner world, called "*nefesh*" in Hebrew, which is commonly referred to as our "life force." It is in this space that we become animated beings with feelings, emotions, opinions, and thoughts. It is here where we feel pleasure and pain, turmoil and success, high and low. It is the arena where the different forces inside us collide, making us experience the push and the pull of our day-to-day life.

Our inner world is compared to a ladder with its feet on the ground and its top reaching up to the heavens, with each rung of the ladder representing a different realm that exists inside of us. Each realm has its own specific set of attributes and properties, each one loftier and more hidden than the one beneath it. The great Kabbalist and philosopher, Rabbi Moshe Chaim Luzzatto, describes in

OUR INNER WORLD IS COMPARED TO A LADDER WITH ITS FEET ON THE GROUND AND ITS TOP REACHING UP TO THE HEAVENS.

our inner world as "having many parts that are bound to each other like links in a chain."[1]

The journey from Egypt to Sinai is a climb from the bottom of the ladder of that inner world—a place of confusion, drama, and turmoil—to the top of the ladder where we can see the world from an elevated view. It is there that we can enjoy a much more joyful, peaceful, and blissful existence as we experience higher states of consciousness, including a greater awareness of the self, the Divine, and a deep sense of clarity and truth. Reaching this high level of consciousness is referred to as *daas* (expanded consciousness) or *d'veikus* (attachment). Throughout our life, we may in fact have experiences that give us a glimpse of these lofty levels, but it is only through climbing the ladder of self-mastery that we can really become deeply connected to this way of life and sustain it in everything that we do.

ALL OUR CHARACTER TRAITS ARE ROOTED IN ONE OF OUR INNER REALMS THAT CORRESPOND TO THE FOUR STATES OF MATTER: FIRE, WIND, WATER, AND EARTH.

The exploration of those rungs was the topic of my book *The Four Elements of an Empowered Life*, and it forms the central theme of this book as well. It is based on a powerful concept taught to us by great Jewish writers throughout the ages (and very much concretized by the great Kabbalist, Rabbi Chaim Vital) that all our character traits are rooted in one of our inner realms that correspond to the four states of matter: fire, wind, water, and earth.

This is because everything that exists in the external world on a macro level is reflected on a micro level inside us, having some expression and manifestation in our inner world. Therefore, when exploring the inner world of man, the various different domains inside us can be said to follow the very same pattern of fire, wind, water, and earth.

The four realms of our inner world each correspond to one of the four material elements in the following way:

---

1 *The Way of God* 3:1.

1. Earth: The Element of Physicality—its primary focus being our survival and servicing our bodily needs.
2. Water: The Element of Emotions—its primary focus is pleasure and connection.
3. Wind: The Element of Thoughts—its primary focus is knowledge and ideas.
4. Fire: The Element of the Will—its primary focus is self-actualization.

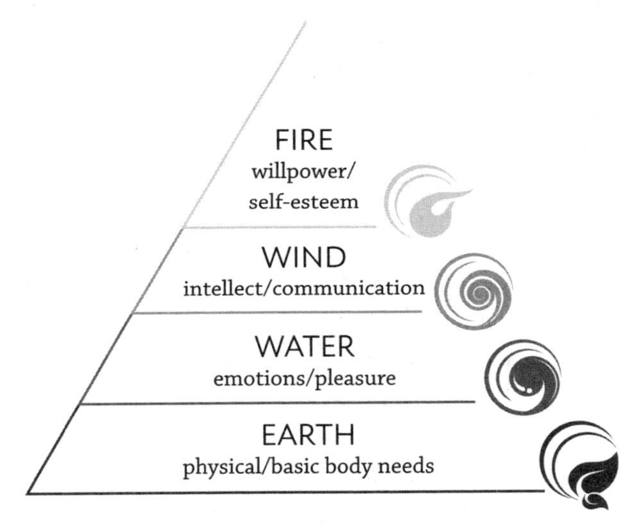

The four elements and their relationship to the four parts of our *nefesh* can also be visualized using the model above. The Earth Element is on the bottom and is the widest because it has the most form and density. As we ascend, form and density diminish, hence it is represented in the shape of a triangle.

The following explanation of our inner realms, which will help us see the four elements in greater depth, is originally found in *The Four Elements of an Empowered Life*:[2]

---

2 Shlomo Buxbaum (Mosaica Press, 2021).

EARTH: THE ELEMENT OF PHYSICALITY

The element of earth is the element that is connected to our physical bodies. At this level, our attention is mostly focused on our bodily needs, and our main drive is for survival and the basic needs that keep our body working and properly maintained, such as the need for food, shelter, and safety. When we are tuned in to this plane of consciousness, the only active parts of our brain are those necessary to sustain our body and keep us alive. We focus on the world and its resources, and even other people, in terms of what they can provide for us.

This level corresponds to earth because just as earth has the most form and the least movement, this part of our consciousness craves security, stability, and consistency, and it takes care of our physical body, which is the densest part of the human being.

WATER: THE ELEMENT OF EMOTION AND DESIRE

Water is the element that corresponds to emotions and desires. At this level, we begin to see beyond just survival, and look for ways to gain pleasure from this journey that we are on. It is here that we begin to experience sophisticated emotions such as love, fear, and hope, as well as lusts and cravings. Human interactions become less transactional, less self-centered, and more about companionship for emotional reasons.

The movement and life-giving power of water is symbolic of the pleasure and emotion that is found at this level. Just as water can be wild and rushing, our emotions can sometimes overwhelm us. However, when we are experiencing healthy emotions, they are like calm waters. The same is true with our desire for pleasure: Sometimes our cravings are raging and intense like the crashing waves, and sometimes they are as subtle as the ocean at low tide.

We often associate our emotions and pleasure with our "heart" because just as the heart pumps oxygen and life throughout the body, our feelings provide us with the vitality to go about our life. It is the pleasure and pain felt at this level that inspires much of our actions.

WIND: THE ELEMENT OF THOUGHT AND COMMUNICATION

Wind is the element connected to our intellect and our ability to communicate. It is here that we seek wisdom, knowledge, understanding, and information to develop the perspectives and direction for our lives. It is driven not by pleasure and emotion, but by logic and sensibility. Feelings are replaced with cognition. Ideas, intuition, and creativity are born. At this level, human relationships center around shared visions and common beliefs, and it is here that our feelings and thoughts are concretized to the point that we can process, articulate, and communicate.

Just like there can be a rapid wind or a calm wind, here, too, our thoughts can be scattered, wild, and, distracting, or they can be calm and blissful. When the winds are rapid, we tend to talk a lot, but when the winds are calm, we experience less need to talk, or feel the need to say only what is necessary.

The thinking/communication level corresponds to wind, which has almost no form and is intangible, just like one's thoughts. The wind also guides the other elements in the same way that the thoughts of a person guide him. It is wind that formulates breath for communication.

FIRE: THE ELEMENT OF WILL AND SELF-IDENTITY

Fire is the spiritual element connected to willpower, self-esteem, and motivation. It is here that our consciousness goes beyond the faculties that are most easily observed and enters into a domain that lies behind many of the decisions that we make and what guides us through life. It is here that our yearning for self-actualization and even greatness is rooted. At this level, we want to feel like we really matter. Feelings and thoughts are replaced with an inner yearning and drive. In our relationships, we feel a responsibility for others as if they are an extension of ourselves.

This level corresponds to fire. The element of fire is the most formless, just as the will is detected least from all the other levels. Just like fire rises up, this level is about that inner yearning to go higher and higher. And just as fire destroys, this is the part of ourselves that we are tapping into when we are trying to overcome obstacles or remove anything blocking us from our path forward.

We have explained the four inner domains of our *nefesh* that correspond to the four elements. However, it would be incorrect to say that we have reached the top of the ladder and that our inner world ends there.

There is indeed a fifth element: our soul. The soul is the essence of who we are. It is referred to as the *nefesh Elokis*, a life-force inside us that is a spark of Godliness. It is an eternal part of us that lives beyond our years in this world. The true "I" is at the soul level. Our body, our emotions, our thoughts, and our will are constantly changing, but we will still be us. That is the highest level.[3]

SLAVE TO THE ELEMENTS

So, what does all of this have to do with the Passover Seder and the four cups of wine?

The Kabbalists refer to the Egyptian bondage as the "slavery of the four elements." This sheds a whole new light on an ancient story. The story, as it was told to us in our youth, painted a picture in our imagination of exhausted slaves carrying heavy bricks on their backs in the hot desert sun while building ancient pyramids. A very sad scene, indeed, but not one that we can apply to our own lives. But there is a much deeper and much more relevant perspective on the entire story, one that sees the entire bondage as interconnected with the four elements.

AT OUR CORE, HUMAN BEINGS DO NOT HAVE PARTS OF US THAT ARE INHERENTLY BAD.

As we mentioned above, these four elements are the roots of all our character traits, and therefore, they are the foundation of our entire life. The "slavery of the four elements," then, means that our very personality was being enslaved, our character was being channeled by an outside influence rather

---

3 The soul itself also has different levels that parallel the four elements. Each of the four elements is connected to an aspect of our soul and, when channeled properly, becomes a vessel for the soul. The Kabbalists give each level of the soul a different name and show how they parallel the lower *nefesh*:

- *Nefesh*—corresponding to the earth element
- *Ruach*—corresponding to the water element
- *Neshamah*—corresponding to the wind element
- *Chayah*—corresponding to the fire element.
- *Yechidah*—corresponding to the Godly soul itself, i.e., the soul of the soul

than our internal compass, and our identity was being manipulated by a more powerful external force.

All character traits, or *middos* in Hebrew—whether in the realm of action, emotion, speech, or thought—can be channeled and expressed in either a positive way or negative way, depending how and when we use them. We often use terms like good character traits and bad traits when referring to how we behave, but at our core, human beings do not have parts of us that are inherently bad. It is only when our character traits are underdeveloped or mischanneled that they are expressed as bad behaviors. When our character traits do not shine in the positive way they are meant to, they are considered "enslaved."

The "slavery of the four elements" is reflected in our own lives when the power of our inner world is being mischanneled, trapping us in a web of negative behavior, emotions, and thoughts. True inner freedom is about being the master of the four elements, accessing the tools for an amazing life. But becoming the master of these realms is not our default mode. Without the hard work to RULE (recognize, understand, learn about, and elevate) over the elements, rather than letting them rule over us, we can go through life making very few real choices. We become slaves to ourselves—our own worst enemies.

The four promises that are represented by the four cups of wine were God's message that the redemption wasn't just from the physical slavery but an elevation of the entire personality and identity of the Jewish People. And it is specifically there that the story of the Exodus becomes more than just our history but our ongoing personal story. It is in the enslavement of the four elements that we can see ourselves as slaves and learn the lessons of how we can free ourselves.

The many ways that we become enslaved to the negative aspects of these elements, and how to channel them positively, will be discussed in detail throughout the book. But in order to really understand how the elements operate inside of us, let's briefly see a few very common examples of how most of us experience a slavery of the four elements:

Let's start with the earth element. Since the earth element is linked to our survival, there is an inner voice inside of us constantly making us aware of our mortality, planting a fear in our mind that our survival is somehow threatened. Hence, much of our life can be spent worrying that something is going to go wrong. We fear death, getting sick, and not having sufficient income and resources to support ourselves.

All of this is normal and healthy, but it can easily be used against us. The reason that the media loves to report bad news is because it is so easy to play on these inner fears and capture our attention with information that will cause us to worry. Once they have exposed this vulnerability, they can use it to exploit us to behave in ways that will ultimately benefit them. The earth element may cause us to become workaholics and neglect our own personal needs or meaningful pursuits because we are afraid of not making enough money or losing our jobs, even when these fears are unfounded. This is how one becomes a slave to the earth element.

Let's move to the water element. It is widely believed that the vast majority of our decisions are made out of a pursuit of pleasure or an avoidance of pain. And most of that is focused on the pain and pleasure of the moment. In fact, people will often assess their entire level of satisfaction with their lives based on how they are feeling at the exact moment you ask them. When we feel emotional pain, we try to drown it out with even more pleasure. Eventually, that pleasure and comfort become habitual for us, even addictive, and we cannot extricate ourselves from it.

Furthermore, our emotional state, i.e., our mood, at any given moment has a shockingly tremendous effect on our decision making in almost every area of life. When we are feeling positive emotions, our decisions are more positive and generous, and we are even more open to taking risks. When we are feeling negative emotions, our decisions will be more constricted, selfish, and conservative. This calls into question our ability to ever make real, rational decisions. Studies have shown that teachers who thought about positive memories before grading tests were more likely to give higher scores![4] And, in a top-tier medical school,

4 Dr. Marc Brackett in his book *Permission to Feel*.

admissions were higher on sunny days, and rejections were higher on rainy days! Clearly, human beings are enslaved by their emotions.

The wind element can also be a source of enslavement. While we are theoretically free to think what we want and express our opinions, the reality is that we are often enslaved by other people's ideas and values that have become ingrained in us either through nurture or from our surrounding environment. Even if we suspect such ideas to be wrong, we are afraid to question those ideologies because of the ramifications if we, in fact, discover them to be wrong. We are unsure whether we are allowed to question those things or even express our confusion. And even if we conclude in our heads that we feel differently from the people around us, we are afraid to communicate that out of the fear of being shunned.

And finally, the fire element is the root of our ego, which is most likely the greatest master of all. If we are not in touch with the things that make us feel authentically worthy, we turn to things that make us feel artificially worthy, like money, power, and materialism. These are all wonderful things if they are an outgrowth of noble pursuits and secondary to what gives us real self-worth. But as ends unto themselves, they could become the source of enslaving the human being. When we do not feel authentically great, we become filled with the fear of humiliation, shame, and disapproval that threatens our sense of worthiness.

THE DARKER SIDE OF THE FOUR ELEMENTS

These are all very general struggles that most of us deal with daily as we are controlled by forces of lower consciousness rather than expanded consciousness. They are coming from a place of weakness and not a place of power. Nothing mentioned above, however, would be characterized as "bad behavior" or "sin." They are just the default mode of decision-making that most of us operate on.

Likely, one wouldn't label them as "bad character," though they are certainly undesirable.

There is, however a much darker side and a more dangerous form of slavery to the four elements. We will see in the upcoming chapters how the four elements can also bring out very negative attributes inside of us. Rooted in each of the elements are character flaws that will emerge if we are not focused on self-mastery, and they will cause us to behave in very damaging ways.

We will discuss those aspects in the upcoming chapters as we begin to explore the specifics of the Egyptian slavery and get to know the villain of the story, Pharaoh.

The redemption from Egypt symbolizes a complete transformation from being enslaved to the darkest parts of our inner world to elevating them and refining the diamond that is inside each of us.

At the Seder, we drink four cups of wine that correspond to the four terms of redemption. The Hebrew word for cup is *kos*, which comes from the same root as the word for "covered up." The four cups are hinting at our four inner worlds that are represented by the four elements. The four terms of redemption are a reminder that we have the ability to RULE over them.

With this important introduction, we are now ready to journey back to Egypt to explore the story anew from this perspective and uncover the magic of a story that we have known since childhood, but perhaps never fully understood.

summary

- The four promises of redemption that God used when informing Moses of the imminent redemption of the Jewish People from Egypt contain within them the entire secret of exile and redemption. They are a roadmap for us and our own personal journey, containing the secret to achieving self-mastery.
- All of our character traits are rooted in one of the four inner realms that make up our *nefesh*, or our "life force." The four inner realms are characterized by the four states of matter: fire, wind, water, and earth.
- Earth is the Element of Physicality with its primary focus being our survival and servicing our body needs. Water is the Element of Emotions with its primary focus being pleasure and connection. Wind is the Element of Thoughts with its primary focus being knowledge and ideas. And Fire is the Element of the Will

with its primary focus being identity self-actualization. There is also a fifth element: our soul.

- The Egyptian bondage was a "slavery of the four elements" and is reflected in our own lives when our attributes are being mischanneled and we feel trapped in a web of negative behavior, emotions, and thoughts. True inner freedom is about being the master of the four elements, accessing the tools for an amazing life.

chapter three

THE INNER PHARAOH AND THE EVIL INCLINATION

MOSES AND PHARAOH: THE STRUGGLES OF THE INNER VOICES

The entertainment industry is very fond of superheroes and supervillains. For the past century, superhero fantasies have captured the imagination of both adults and children in comic books and on the screen, bringing in billions of dollars of revenue each year as the most profitable genre of entertainment. But superheroes and villains are not a new phenomenon. For all of history, fictitious and mythological tales of good forces with superpowers defending the world from horrific bad forces trying to wreak havoc have captured people's imaginations.

The psychology of superheroes is very deep. It's more than just the colorful outfits, artwork, and special effects. There is something there that resonates with us. There is deep psychological truth to the struggle between good and evil, as it reflects the ongoing inner struggle with which we all must contend.

Like the superhero, we know that we, too, possess something hidden and special inside of us that we can unlock to help us defeat whatever force of negativity with which we are contending. Superheroes who discover their superpowers after thinking that they are just regular people are especially exciting for us because it awakens in us the hope that maybe, somehow, we have some hidden superpower that we just haven't yet discovered. It gives us hope that, any day now, we might just discover it, and our entire life may change!

When one begins to explore the depth of Torah, there is no longer a need to turn to fiction, fantasy, or mythology. The Torah itself tells the story of our ancestors and those who tried to harm us. But within each of those personas, there is the archetype of a deeper attribute, a part of us that is waiting to be unleashed. The great patriarchs, matriarchs, and leaders of the Torah all represent shining lights within our own inner world that can light up our life when given proper expression. And their enemies represent the dark side of our personalities that exist to challenge us and derail us from accomplishing our holy mission.

As we explore the story of the Exodus as a model for leaving our personal places of constraint, we want to look at the Torah personalities who are at the center of the story and see them as archetypes for different personas that exist within us.

Two major personas emerge from the story, setting the stage for a showdown between good and evil: Moses on the side of good, and Pharaoh on the side of bad. These two opposing personalities are meant to be understood as two opposing forces inside of us: one force trying to keep us stuck in the struggles of today, and another trying to liberate us and lead us to our potential.

Jewish tradition frames the inner struggle between right and wrong, good and bad, dark and light, holy and unholy, etc., as the battling voices of two inner personas referred to as the *yetzer tov*, "the good inclination," and the *yetzer hara*, "the evil inclination." Our constant struggle boils down to the push and pull that happens between these two inner forces. This is the inner Moses and Pharaoh that exists inside of us.[1]

THE INNER VOICE OF POSITIVITY AND SPIRITUALITY INSIDE OF US OFTEN STRUGGLES TO MAKE ITSELF KNOWN, TO HAVE ITS VOICE HEARD.

The name "Pharaoh" contains the very same letters that can be broken up into *peh ra*, meaning evil speech, hinting to that inner voice inside of us that is trying to trick or deceive us. Moses, on the other hand, was famous for having a *k'vad peh*, heavy speech, indicating an inability to properly express

1 *Rambam* (Maimonidies), *Michtav Hameyuchas LaRambam:* "Pharaoh, King of Egypt, is the evil inclination. Moses is Divine wisdom."

himself. This speaks to the fact that the inner voice of positivity and spirituality inside of us often struggles to make itself known, to have its voice heard.

The struggle between the *yetzer tov* and the *yetzer hara* is so commonly referenced within Jewish literature, and so much a part of the messaging of Judaism, that even the youngest of children will reference it and understand that they have these two forces inside of them. But like many other deep concepts in the area of spirituality, when a concept becomes second nature to us, we often neglect to fully explore it in its depth with all its nuance. Much of our success in combating the *yetzer hara* comes down to a greater self-awareness and an understanding of how we work. Our goal is not to let Pharaoh rule over us, but to learn how to RULE over him by fully Recognizing, Understanding, and Learning about our *yetzer hara* so that we can Elevate it.

GET TO KNOW YOUR YETZER HARA

Who or what is this *yetzer hara* inside of us? Where does it reside, and how are we to recognize it when it rears its ugly head?

We have many images and ideas floating around our imagination depicted by childhood tales and the entertainment industry, such as the little white angel with wings and a halo standing above our right shoulder trying to dissuade us from the awful advice of the devilish-looking red angel holding a pitchfork, standing above our left shoulder and encouraging us to wreak havoc and do terrible things. These images don't quite align with the Jewish view of things.

As we look toward Jewish tradition to try to understand what this force is, we find that two different pictures emerge.

At times, our Sages will equate the *yetzer hara* with some sort of evil external force, such as the Satan,[2] the Angel of Death, or the snake who

---

2 It is important to note here that Judaism does not view "Satan" with the same implications as other religions. The Hebrew word *satan* can be translated as "opponent," "accuser," or to "turn away." Rather than being an autonomous force, or a devilish, rebellious angel, as in other religions, Judaism views Satan as a messenger of God, here to carry out God's purpose to present us with challenges along our path. This provides us with free-will choices to make and an opportunity to be the creator of our destiny. In Kabbalah, the Satan is synonymous

tempted Adam and Eve in the Garden of Eden. This force seems to live outside of us but comes to pay us a visit throughout the day, manipulating the events of our life in a way that it will provide us challenges and temptations.

Our Sages go as far as to say that "a person does not sin unless a spirit of folly enters into him." It is as if they are implying that a negative force exists that can enter into us, possessing us to sin in a manner that is beyond what we really want for ourselves and in ways that we certainly know better. Many who are suffering with a bad habit or addiction can relate to this. No matter how badly they want to stop, no matter how many times they have promised themselves that they would never return to their harmful path, they continue to fall trap to the behavior. At some point, they might say, "I am no longer in control. It is as if something takes hold of me whenever I am confronted with this temptation."

Elsewhere, though, a different picture emerges of the *yetzer hara*. Our Sages see a fascinating reference to the evil inclination in the words of the Torah that are written shortly after the creation of man, when the Torah says, "Behold, it was *very* good." The Midrash comments:

> *"Behold, it was good" refers to the yetzer tov, the Good Inclination; "And behold, it was very good" refers to the yetzer hara, the Evil Inclination. Can the Evil Inclination be very good? That would be extraordinary! But without the Evil Inclination, however, no man would build a house, take a wife, and beget children.*[3]

It seems from here that the *yetzer hara* is not an external force, but an inner drive that is naturally inclined toward material success, pleasure, and building a legacy. Without proper guidance, this can lead to

---

with an angel named Sama'el, and is represented in the Torah by the snake in the Garden of Eden, the Angel of Death, and the ministering angel of the nation of Amalek that will be discussed later in this book. Kabbalah also refers to the Satan as the *Sitra Achra*—literally "the other side"—because he is rooted in God's attribute of justice.

3 *Bereishis Rabbah* 9:7.

evil, but when properly controlled, it will drive a person to accomplish some of the great life milestones that are necessary for building up the physical world.

This is also the implication of another verse in the Torah, referencing the evil inclination by saying that "the heart of man is evil from his youth." Our Sages echo this verse by saying that "for the first thirteen years [of a person's life], the *yetzer hara* is greater than the *yetzer tov*. There, in his mother's womb, a person's evil urge grows with him. After thirteen years, the good urge is born."[4]

I have had the great pleasure of holding my children when they are first born. They are so innocent and pure. All they really want to do is eat and feel secure. Where is the evil in that? And sure, we have had our share of ups and downs like all parents. We have sent our kids to their rooms, given them consequences, and gotten calls from their teachers. But to say that their evil urge is greater than their urge to do good seems to be a bit of an overstatement.

But, as said, this "evil" urge being referenced here is not necessarily an urge to blow things up or commit grave sins, but rather is the desire to feel secure, to discover pleasure, to think independently, and to matter. In contrast to the *yetzer tov*, which is purely spiritual in nature, desiring none of those material matters, the *yetzer hara* is more attracted to the material aspects of life that make this earthly journey more safe and more pleasurable. If the *yetzer tov* was the sole voice within a person, he would lack interest in the physical world, causing the person to become an ascetic and be completely removed from the world. The balance of these two inner forces is what allows us to oscillate between these two worlds—to be both physical and spiritual beings in one body in one lifetime.

It is this aspect of the *yetzer hara* that begins to develop from the time the baby leaves the womb, getting a solid thirteen-year head start to the *yetzer tov*. For without that head start, the pristine voice of the *yetzer tov* showing them the brilliance of spiritual connection in their

---

4 *Avos D'Rabi Nosson* 16.

early years would certainly overpower their material desires and hinder the child from ever tasting true free will. If the *yetzer hara* would not be given the advantage of time, then the deep yearning of our hearts to grow closer to God would completely overpower it, and it would stand no chance.[5]

DEFINING EVIL

Hence, we see two very different pictures of the *yetzer hara* emerging: the outer force of evil and the inner drive that can be elevated. In an attempt to reconcile these seemingly different understandings of the *yetzer hara* and the human condition, the great master of personal development, Rav Yisrael Salanter explains that there are actually two different forces of evil present in a person:

- *Yetzer hara* #1 is the kind of evil that is an outer force, an angel perhaps, who convinces a person to do evil, like the snake in the Garden of Eden that came to persuade Adam and Eve to eat from the Tree of Knowledge.
- *Yetzer hara* #2 is an inner voice of struggle that is enmeshed in our very heart, causing us to have physical desires and urges but that can be elevated for good when it partners together with another inner force, the *yetzer tov*. This is the level of consciousness that was internalized in the Garden of Eden when Adam and Eve ate from the Tree of Knowledge.[6]

Both *yetzer hara* #1 and #2 are crucial parts of the Divine masterplan, setting the stage for us to live a life of free will and choice. *Yetzer hara* #1 must be conquered. *Yetzer hara* #2 must be properly channeled. But both are messengers of God, and both exist for our benefit.

According to this perspective of the *yetzer hara*, one might wonder why we refer to it as the "evil" inclination. Surely, the desire to build a house, get married, have children, and enjoy the pleasure of the material world should not be identified as evil!

---

5 *Chovos Halevavos, Shaar Avodas HaElokim*, chap. 2.

6 *Igeres Hamussar*.

The answer is that the word "evil" is actually not the most accurate definition of the word *ra*. The very same letters that make up the word *ra* (*reish* [ר] and *ayin* [ע]) are also the two letters that form the word for friend (*rei'a*) and shepherd (*ro'eh*). In Jewish thought, words that share a root will have a deep connection between them, even if their obvious translations may not seem that way. What might be the thread that weaves together these three themes: friendship, shepherding, and something connected with evil?

Let's toss another word into the mix that also has these root letters that just may give us the final clue. On Rosh Hashanah, the Torah tells us to sound the shofar with a blast that is referred to as a *teruah*, a word that also derives from the same root. It is a blast that contains a series of broken sounds.

Perhaps you have realized that this is indeed the key to solving this puzzle: the theme of brokenness. All of the words imply that something is broken. Friendship is built on the fact that two human beings can come together to support each other in hard times—to complete each other. Like pieces of a puzzle that click together in the areas when one shape is lacking and the other has extra, friendships are formed as a way for two people to support one another in their brokenness.

A shepherd takes a flock of independent sheep who would each be doing their own thing, going in their own direction, and unites them together into one flock. Once again, taking the pieces of the puzzle and putting them together to form a greater picture.

And finally, the "evil" inclination called the *yetzer hara*. Calling our inner world "evil" is part of a script that is foreign to Judaism. Calling our inner world "broken" is much more accurate. Our material desires are naturally disconnected from our deepest spiritual yearnings. Left alone, they can make us lose focus of what is truly valuable, and what we truly desire. Left alone, our *yetzer hara* leads us down a path where all of our pursuits feel disjointed, lacking a unity of purpose. This is the brokenness we may often feel in our life. But brokenness means that it can be repaired. Brokenness is a temporary state. Brokenness means that we have all of the pieces, and they just need to be put together. We can transform the *ra*, the brokenness, of our inner world to *rei'a*, a friend, a part of us that can be elevated. It is no coincidence that Moses, who is symbolic of the *yetzer tov*, was a *ro'eh*, a shepherd, at the time that he was chosen. Moses in the story of the Exodus, and the *yetzer tov* in our personal story, represent the ability to gather together all of the broken pieces inside of us and put them together to create a new and beautiful whole.

MOSES IN THE STORY OF THE EXODUS, AND THE YETZER TOV IN OUR PERSONAL STORY, REPRESENT THE ABILITY TO GATHER TOGETHER ALL OF THE BROKEN PIECES INSIDE OF US AND PUT THEM TOGETHER TO CREATE A NEW AND BEAUTIFUL WHOLE.

BACK TO MOSES AND PHARAOH

We can now return to our understanding of how the battle between Moses and Pharaoh is supposed to represent our inner struggles.

The Torah teaches that Moses first encounters God at the bush that was aflame but not consumed by the fire. God gives Moses the important charge of returning to Egypt and liberating the Jewish People. Moses protests on many accounts—he is unworthy, he won't be listened to, and he has a hard time speaking, so Pharaoh certainly won't listen to him. This represents the idea that we said above that the *yetzer tov* is still and silent in the early years of our development. Slowly, we fall into the slavery of Pharaoh, the evil inclination, the Mitzrayim of our early years. Over time, we mature to the point that we are ready to enter into the fight. But the *yetzer tov* is quiet at first and needs lots of persuasion.

God gives Moses a sign to perform for Pharaoh and then for the Jewish People: He will throw down his staff and it will be transformed into a snake and back. Kabbalah teaches that this staff represents the Tree of Knowledge of Good and Evil. God was therefore saying to Moses: "This staff will be used to perform great miracles; it will be the sign of freedom. It can also turn into a snake, the force of evil from the Garden of Eden, but only temporarily." The message that Moses is meant to convey to Pharaoh, who believes that he is the owner of the Jewish People, and to the Jewish People, who may no longer believe in themselves, is that their state of enslavement is only a mirage. They are a holy people whose transformation back to holiness is imminent.

The four elements are the battle ground. It is the battlefield on which all of our inner wars are fought. They can be elevated and used to climb the ladder to discover our highest possible selves. Or they can be taken and corrupted. Pharaoh is symbolic of that force of negativity, the snake that tries to corrupt them and enslave them in Mitzrayim, a place of constraint, challenging us in different ways on each of these levels.

THE FOUR CORRUPTIONS OF HUMAN CHARACTER

Rabbi Chaim Vital says that each of these elements is the root of one of the four main character struggles from which every person must constantly strive to refine himself. They are the following:

1. Sluggishness (including laziness, sadness, unworthiness, and jealousy etc.)—connected to the Earth Element
2. Lust—connected to the Water Element
3. Levity (trivial and corrupt thoughts and words)—connected to the Wind Element
4. Arrogance—connected to the Fire Element

They are connected to the four inner elements in the following way:

- The Earth/Body level is the root of sluggishness and laziness, just as the earth itself is dense and lacks any movement. The heaviness of earth is also represented in the heaviness that we feel throughout our life when we feel stuck, not accomplishing anything, or just burned out. Because the earth/body level is mainly concerned about survival, we feel anxious and concerned about the future, sometimes for no real reason at all. This contributes further to our sad and heavy state, and it also leads us to become jealous of others who we perceive as having it better than we do.
- The Water/Emotion level is the root of both an endless pursuit of pleasure, including forbidden pleasures and lusts, and also unhealthy indulgence in things that are allowed. Both feelings of love as well as physical pleasures activate related areas in our brains, known as pleasure centers. The movement and life-giving power of water represents our desire to experience the pleasures of life.

- The Wind/Intellectual/Communication level becomes the root of levity, falsehood, and corruption of speech. The blowing of the wind represents the constant flow of thoughts through our head, which can either be meaningful or silly thoughts. Wind also represents the breath that is contained in our words: A meaningful mind will produce meaningful speech, while a frivolous mind will produce frivolous speech.
- The Fire/Will level becomes the root of inflated ego and an endless desire to be shown honor and respect. Fire that rises to the top represents our desire for self-actualization and to feel important. A person who becomes obsessed with his own self-worth will struggle with haughtiness and excessive pride.

We now have the tools to understand with depth and clarity the deeper message of the Jewish nation being born in exile in Egypt. We established earlier that the Jewish People were going through a refinement process like precious metal in a furnace. This refinement process was to extract from them the impurities from the first two thousand years of mankind, specifically in regard to the corruption of the four elements, as we will soon see. The corruption of these early generations, who set the foundation of mankind, formed the "spiritual DNA" of all generations to come. To reawaken the holy potential would require a major refining process.

In the upcoming chapters, we will explore this in greater detail. We will show how these four negative attributes that are the corruption of the four elements were all trademark characteristics of the land of Egypt. We will take a closer look at what the Jewish People had to witness and endure in the land of Egypt and in the lifestyle of Pharaoh and the Egyptians, and see how the four human flaws manifested there. We will also explore how they reflect the early flaws of humankind that the Jewish People were there to refine. In doing so, we will see how the Torah is actually a blueprint for our own inner world and personal struggles.

As part of our mission in this world, we are here to refine our inner world and conquer our inner realms by transforming these negative traits and using each of our elements for the positive. This is our work in this world, and this was the primary reason that the Jewish nation needed to go through the Egyptian exile.

summary

- The battle between Moses and Pharaoh is symbolic of the two opposing forces inside of us. The *yetzer hara*, or evil inclination, is a force trying to keep us stuck in the struggles of today. The *yetzer tov* is a force that is trying to liberate us and lead us to our potential.
- There are two aspects to the evil inclination. The first is an external force that manipulates the events of our lives to provide us challenges and temptations. The other is an inner drive that can be properly channeled and elevated. The four inner elements can be corrupted and elevated. When they are being corrupted, they are under the influence of Pharaoh, i.e., the evil inclination.
- The four main character struggles from which every person must constantly strive to refine himself are: sluggishness (including laziness, sadness, depression, etc.), connected to the Earth Element; lust, connected to the Water Element; levity (wasting time/words with trivial matters), connected to the Wind Element; and arrogance, connected to the Fire Element.

chapter four

FEELING STUCK IN EARTHINESS

ELEMENT	THE STRUGGLE	THE ORIGIN
Earth	Sluggishness, sadness	Cain and Abel

THE THREE CAUSES OF AN UNSATISFACTORY LIFE

Let us begin to dive deeper into understanding the elements and their connection to Egypt by exploring the element of earth, the element of physicality, the struggles associated with it, and how it relates to the Jewish People's enslavement in Egypt.

It is no secret that most people struggle with some level of discontent with their life. We all go through our ups and downs. It seems that many people, however, spend a lot more time on the downside of things. As time goes on, the overall mental and emotional health of society is declining, as more and more people feel that life is no more than a big rat race to nowhere.

As kids, we dreamed of the freedom that we would have as adults. As adults, we yearn for the freedom that we had as children. The bills that come in at the end of the month keep us chained to our desks. There is this underpinning of fear and anxiety lurking somewhere between our bellies and our throats, a voice in our head constantly nagging us that no matter how good we have it today, it can only be a matter of time until it all collapses.

As our insecurity grows, we try to drown out those anxious feelings by constantly occupying ourselves with activities that will give us the sense that we are being very responsible and building a secure future. More work. Less calm. We take on more and more things to do until we completely forget that we have a life and an identity that is not connected to our jobs, errands, and tasks. We are now chained to a vicious cycle of living to work rather than working to live. And when we do have moments that we should be able to enjoy with our families and our children, we struggle to be fully present.

We see how large portions of society swap movement for coffee, reading for screen time, and fresh air for the office air freshener. So many hard-working people collapse into bed at night completely exhausted, only to sluggishly roll out of bed in the morning and schlep their feet into the new day. They dread the new day because of the fear of failure that it brings with it. Life feels as if it is lacking higher purpose, and so much energy is being swallowed up by maintenance and just trying to survive. Even when there is no work left to be done, the life of the average person outside of work feels quite boring—so much so that he will either throw himself into pointless activities as an escape, or back into work to temporarily relieve the anxiety.

Many of us wonder how our life compares to everyone else's. We make assumptions that other people are happier, more productive, and more successful. We see the pictures of other people's life highlights, and though we know that we are only getting a specifically curated snapshot of their world, it still feels like they are doing a better job navigating the roller coaster of life. And instead of being happy for them, we often become resentful and jealous.

EARTH IS PREDICTABLE AND RELIABLE, AND WE CERTAINLY NEED A LOT OF THAT IN OUR LIFE. BUT WHEN WE BECOME STUCK IN IT, OUR LIFE RESEMBLES THE LIFE OF A SLAVE.

This is the description of those who are experiencing an excess of earthiness in their life. It is dense, heavy, and a massive burden. Hopefully, it is nothing more than an exaggerated version of your own life, but you probably found some truth there. The earth element is a helpful tool when the focus on our mortality leads us to be productive, seek stability, and maintain a set routine in our life. Earth is predictable and reliable, and we certainly need a lot of that in our life. But when we become stuck in it, our life resembles the life of a slave.

The description above of the challenges of the earth element is represented by the hard work and slavery that Pharaoh imposed on the Jewish People. Our Sages teach us that when the Torah tells us of the "hard work" that the Jewish People suffered at Pharaoh's hand, his main goal was to drain their vitality. This was more important than the actual structures that they were being asked to build. In fact, according to our Sages, the cities that they were asked to build, Pithom and Raamses, were unsuitable land to build on, and the structures did not last; they either toppled over or were swallowed into quicksand.[1]

Pharaoh also understood that as long as the Jewish People have even the smallest amount of off-duty time, they will use it to meditate, to study Torah, or just to think a little about life. He understood that these few moments would be a source of vitality for the Jewish People and would ensure their continuity. So, the goal was to keep them busy at every moment. This is a common symptom of the culture that we live in, where we wear "being busy" as a status symbol.

Additionally, the Egyptian taskmasters made sure that every Jew was engaged in a task that was not properly suited for his skills. The Egyptians understood that the key to demoralizing a person is to deprive him of the ability to properly express his talents.

We learn from these tactics of enslavement three tendencies of the earth element that may occur in our own life:

- The lack of a feeling of accomplishment and advancement in one's life
- A constant feeling of pressure and busyness just to keep up with the whirlwind of life
- The feeling that our natural talents and gifts are not being properly utilized or matched to the tasks in which we are engaged

In contrast to this, let's take a look at how our Sages describe the beginning of Moses's "career" as a leader.[2] Keep in mind that Moses

---

1 *Sotah* 11a.
2 *Shemos Rabbah* 1:28.

is the symbol for our good consciousness, the positive voice that lives inside of us.

First, the Midrash comments on the Torah's statement that Moses "saw them in their burdens":

> *For he would look upon their burdens and cry and say, "Woe is me unto you...for there is not more difficult labor than the labor of the mortar."*

In modern language, we would call that "validation." For the one who is feeling unaccomplished, who is feeling down on himself, can there be a more comforting voice than one that says, "I see you. I feel you. What you are doing is tremendous!"?

The Midrash then goes on to say how he supported them:

> *If he saw a large burden on a small person, and a small burden on a large person, or a man's burden on a woman, and a woman's burden on a man, or an elderly man's burden on a young man, and a young man's burden on an elderly man, he would leave his rank and go and right their burdens.*

This was more than an act of easing a burden that was too heavy for someone; it also included giving someone a heavier burden if he could handle it. This was to ensure that people would feel their talents being properly utilized.

The Midrash goes on:

> *He went and said to Pharaoh, "One who has a slave, if he does not rest one day a week, he will die! While your slaves, if you don't allow them rest one day a week, they will die!" He said to them, "Go and do for them as you are saying." Moses went and established the Shabbat day for them to rest.*

Someone who never stops working, who can't shut down, is living a life of slavery. Moses ensured that the Jewish People could keep the Shabbat so that they could recharge and recalibrate. In addition to the importance of observing Shabbat for spiritual reasons, the Midrash here is focusing on the importance of managing one's time so that he has time for the important things in life.

As we battle the inherent tendency to feel down from time to time about life, it would benefit us greatly to learn these lessons to shift our focus to a better place and increase our vitality:

- Work toward a very specific goal—something you would like to accomplish that is doable, measurable, and can be completed within a certain time-frame. Keep a running journal of every accomplishment along the way—both big and small.
- Make the shifts and tweaks in your life to do more of the things that fit your natural skills and abilities. Try to outsource and delegate tasks that drain your energy. Be open and honest with people when you are not the best suited to deliver a specific result.
- Establish clear boundaries with your time. When is it time to work? When is it time to give to others? When is it time to recharge?

THE ORIGIN OF EARTHINESS

As mentioned above, the enslavement in Egypt was to refine the flaws of the early generations that became part of the spiritual DNA of humanity. The root of the struggle of earthiness can be traced all the way back to the earliest stories of mankind.

After eating from the Tree of Knowledge, God curses Adam that "with sadness" he would eat from the earth, and that through the "sweat of his brow" he would eat his bread.[3]

---

3 There is a very significant literary connection here between the early generations and the Egyptian exile. Part of the curse of Adam that is channeled toward the earth is that it will grow thorns and thistles, "*kotz v'dardar*." The severity of the curse of earth lasts for the next era of mankind until the time of Noach, who the Torah says brought comfort to the world from the "thorns and thistles of the ground" (through his inventions). The very language that the Torah uses to describe the Egyptians' frustration with the Jewish People reminds us of that curse: "The [Egyptians] became disgusted (*va'yakutzu*) by the Israelites." The term "*va'yakutzu*" is interpreted by the Midrash as "they were like thorns."

The story of Cain killing Abel, which immediately follows the story of Eden, continues to highlight this struggle of the earth element. Embracing the curse of the land, Cain commits himself to becoming a "worker of **the earth**," both in the literal and metaphorical sense. When the two brothers bring an offering to God, Cain is stingy with his offering, and God only accepts Abel's. At this point, Cain experiences intense jealousy and depression, two traits strongly associated with the earth element. He quarrels with his brother and murders him. God decrees that Cain must live a life of exile, and the earth is further cursed.

The very same insecurity and anxiety that caused Cain to turn against his brother also brings the Egyptians to turn against their Jewish neighbors:

> *A new king arose over Egypt who did not know Joseph. And he said to his people, "Look, the Israelite people are much too numerous for us. Let us deal shrewdly with them so that they may not increase; otherwise, in the event of war, they may join our enemies in fighting against us and rise from the ground."*

The first thing we may notice is the sudden change of Pharaoh's heart. Everything seems to be going well in the land of Egypt. Jews and Egyptians are getting along very nicely. Then, Pharaoh gets this pit in his stomach that something is going wrong. Suddenly, the book of Exodus is starting to sound quite similar to the beginning of the book of Genesis. The two brothers, Cain and Abel, have the whole world to share, and yet all Cain can see is how Abel is a threat to him. There is no more room for the two of them.

The earth element is uncomfortable with any sort of instability, even when it is in the form of positive growth. When things in life are going smoothly, we would expect to feel content and calm. And yet, out of nowhere, inner voices arise that tell us that there is something wrong—that there is a problem. The inner voice of the earth element starts to create stories inside our head and, suddenly, everyone and everything is out to get us. The Jewish nation had been faithful and patriotic citizens, yet suddenly they became the bad guys. The earth element doesn't allow us to see a bigger picture. Instead, we start feeling all sorts of insecurities, projecting them onto others.

In the words of Russ Harris, in *The Happiness Trap*:

> *We are hardwired to suffer psychologically: to compare, evaluate, and criticize ourselves, to focus on what we're lacking, to rapidly become dissatisfied with what we have, and to imagine all sorts of frightening scenarios, most of which will never happen. No wonder humans find it hard to be happy!*

It is because of this natural tendency to focus on what we are missing that it is becoming increasingly common for people who truly want to be happy to establish a daily gratitude practice, usually as part of their morning routine, where they direct their focus through meditation and journaling on the things in their life for which they should have gratitude. People who consciously count their blessings live happier and more joy-filled lives, and live with a greater state of well-being. Many who have such practices claim that the more that they practice gratitude, the more they start seeing throughout their day additional things for which they should have gratitude.

PEOPLE WHO CONSCIOUSLY COUNT THEIR BLESSINGS LIVE HAPPIER AND MORE JOY-FILLED LIVES, AND LIVE WITH A GREATER STATE OF WELL-BEING.

In Jewish practice, beginning one's day with gratitude is a built-in part of the morning prayers. The very first line in the morning prayers is *Modeh Ani*. The prayers then go on to a section filled with blessings that acknowledge all the aspects of our life that we are meant to recognize are from God, including our bodily functions, our souls, our ability to see, to stand upright, and to move.

SOUL CONNECTIONS

There is yet another fascinating connection between Cain and Abel, the Jews in Egypt, and the earth element. This occurs the first time that we are reintroduced to Moses as an adult. The Torah does not give us any information about Moses's day-to-day activities, his personality, or any other information besides for this interesting story:

> *When Moses had grown up, he went out to his kinsfolk and witnessed their labors. He saw an Egyptian beating a Hebrew, one of his kinsmen. He turned this way and that, and seeing no one about, he struck down the Egyptian and hid him in the sand.*

The ancient wisdom of Kabbalah teaches us that there are soul connections between different personalities that may span different generations. This means that a personality who falls short at one point in history might be connected to a personality later in time with very similar struggles. This "reincarnation" may be able to bring about a *tikkun*, a spiritual rectification, through their overcoming the struggle or receiving a consequence for it.

The beginning of the corruption of the earth element happened when Cain killed his brother and buried him in the earth in a pure act of jealousy toward his brother. Moses's initiation as a leader came about through his defending "a brother" and burying the Egyptian attacker in the earth. According to Kabbalistic teachings, this Egyptian had a soul connection to Cain, and the confrontation between Moses (who was a reincarnation of Abel) and the Egyptian was meant to symbolize the beginning of the rectification of the earth element that was corrupted by the early generations and, more specifically, by Cain.

However, something went wrong. The verses continue:

> *When he went out the next day, he found two Hebrews fighting; so he said to the offender, "Why do you strike your fellow?" He retorted, "Who made you chief and ruler over us? Do you mean to kill me as you killed the Egyptian?" Moses was frightened, and thought: Then the matter is known!*

Moses saw that there was still jealousy and senseless hatred that comes from the earth element. Based on this, he realized that the time for the redemption still had not arrived.

SCARCITY VS. ABUNDANCE

How can one move beyond this earthiness that we have described above?

In modern-day psychology, the term for this type of attitude that breeds the corruption of the earth element, i.e., the behavior of Cain and of the Egyptians, is referred to as "scarcity mindset," the opposite of an "abundance mindset." With a scarcity mindset, a person is always feeling insecure about the future, focused on his limitations, and feeling down about his productivity. Furthermore, other people become threats, causing feelings of jealousy and hostility to arise.

Abundance mindset fosters the opposite. We become confident and optimistic about our future. We are realistic about the possibility that challenges may arise, but we believe that we have the ability to deal with whatever comes our way. Everything can be figured out, and the best is yet to come. We are then able to see our lives and see others in a positive light, and we are flooded with generosity and gratitude toward others.

As we will see later in the book, one of the great miracles of the Exodus was the great change of heart that so many Egyptians had when the Jewish People were leaving Egypt. Instead of the "thorn in the side" mentality, the Egyptians showered the Jewish People with gifts and riches as they were leaving Egypt—a beautiful expression of the redemption of the earth element.

Elevating our mindset is the first step to channeling the earth element in a positive direction. It is the first step to breaking the shackles of sluggishness and sadness. And it is completely in our power to do. Spending some time each day focusing on gratitude and our accomplishments will upgrade our mindset. Becoming aware when we are looking at ourselves as victims of our life, rather than the creators of it, and replacing those thoughts with more empowering ones will transform our experience of the world around us.

summary

- The earth element causes a person to view their life as a constant burden, uninspired by their pursuits, and lacking the feeling of accomplishment. This is represented by the hard work and slavery that Pharaoh imposed on the Jewish People.

- This inherent satisfaction is rooted in the sin of Adam and Eve when God cursed Adam. The story of Cain killing Abel that immediately follows the story of Eden continues to highlight this struggle of the earth element, as Cain experiences intense jealousy and depression, two traits that are strongly associated with the earth element.
- In modern-day psychology, this is referred to as the "scarcity mindset" and is the opposite of an "abundance mindset." With a scarcity mindset, a person is always feeling insecure about the future, focused on his limitations, and feeling down about his productivity. Furthermore, other people become threats, causing feelings of jealousy and hostility to arise. Abundance mindset fosters the opposite, empowering us to become confident and optimistic about the possibilities of life.

chapter five

SWIMMING IN THE WATERS OF DESIRE

ELEMENT	THE STRUGGLE	THE ORIGIN
Water	Forbidden desires	Generation of the Flood

PLEASURE AND PASSION

Our discussion now moves to the element of water, the element of pleasure and connection. Here, too, we will discover the struggles associated with it, and how it relates to the Jewish People's enslavement in Egypt.

A short while ago, a well-known dating, marriage, and intimacy coach was a guest on my weekly podcast to speak about her work and about the Jewish tools to keep the spark in marriage alive. She told me about a client of hers who was in a marriage that was falling apart. Her husband was working extremely hard, and by the time he would arrive home each night, he would be too exhausted and drained to give his wife the proper attention. She wanted to talk, but he was all "talked out" for the day and just wanted to zone out. She, in turn, started drifting farther and farther away from him, leaving the marriage in an emotionless state.

As they began to grow emotionally apart, the passion and physical attraction in their marriage also began to dwindle, to the point that she felt like they were just roommates. Both spouses started to believe that they were no longer in love with one another and began contemplating separation.

For those readers who have been married for some time and whose social circles have many years of marriage under their belt, this story may sound all too familiar. This is such a common experience that it is likely that someone in your circle may be going through the same thing. Even the younger readers as well may not be surprised by this story, as marriage in modern society is often portrayed in media as being a road that leads to monotony, boredom, and lacks the spontaneity and excitement that young couples feel for one another. This would explain why marriage rates are down, young people are waiting longer to get married, if they even marry, and divorce rates are climbing.

THE ELEMENT OF WATER FOSTERS IN US BOTH A POSITIVE YEARNING FOR LOVE AND CONNECTION, AS WELL AS THE NEGATIVE PULL TOWARD PHYSICAL GRATIFICATION.

But don't worry, the story above has a happy ending. After realizing that she did not want to watch her marriage dissolve, she committed to saving the marriage using the power of...water! But to fully appreciate the beauty of the end of this story, which we will see shortly, let us first delve into a deeper understanding of the water element and how to elevate it, rather than to become enslaved by it.

The water element is the source of our desire for pleasure, and it can be channeled toward deep loving relationships or be channeled toward forbidden lust and overindulgence. The following idea, originally presented in *The Four Elements of an Empowered Life*, will help us understand this connection.

> *The element of water fosters in us both a positive yearning for love and connection, as well as the negative pull toward physical gratification...Just as water is the source of all life and growth, it is the love and connection that we feel that is the source of all our vitality. When we feel loved, we feel a great sense of pleasure. Just as our bodies are about sixty-percent water, our inner life-force is powered by the spiritual element of water, the love and connection that we feel.*
>
> *Still, the reverse of this is also true. When we feel that we are lacking love and connection, we begin to feel a strong inner*

> *emptiness, and our brains look for an easy way to substitute the drought that is caused by our loneliness. We naturally gravitate toward substituting that desire for pleasure with other pleasurable experiences that give us a "quick fix," fooling our brains to temporarily think that everything is good. This can lead us to indulge in excess pleasure and generate feelings of lust and inappropriate desires.*
>
> *Water only provides life and goodness when in the proper measure and when properly channeled. An overflow of water, however, can bring destruction and devastation to the world. This is true about physical pleasure as well. When we indulge in physical pleasure more and more with no boundaries at all, it turns to lust and obsession. It becomes a distraction, hurts our pride, and zaps our energy, eventually turning into an unhealthy habit or addiction. The inner pure desire to feel love and connection is replaced with an unquenchable thirst for more physical pleasure.*

Egypt is deeply connected with the element of water. Geographically, this is because it sits on the bank of the Nile, which would overflow its banks. There is deep symbolism here as well. Our Sages teach us that Egypt was steeped in immorality. If we look back at all the Torah's previous accounts, Egypt has already built up a reputation. We remember how in Genesis, when Abraham and Sarah made their way into Egypt during a famine, their main concern was how the Egyptians were going to see Sarah's beauty and take her for their own pleasure—a concern that indeed ended up being fulfilled. We are also reminded of Joseph's first experience in Egypt when, after being sold as a slave, his master's wife tried to seduce him.

It seems that whenever we hear about Egypt, discussion of immoral behavior is not far behind.

Throughout the Torah, when the discussion arises of immoral behavior, the immorality is often described as "the immoralities of Egypt." Scrolls and paintings discovered from that period also leave that impression, as they visually depict various immoral acts that were practiced in

Egypt.[1] Furthermore, our Sages teach that Goshen, the location where the Jewish People originally settled, experienced the greatest decline in morality during that period.[2] Jewish families had to live side-by-side with their lustful Egyptian neighbors, fighting hard to maintain their holiness and purity.

Part of the challenge of the exile was to empower the Jewish People to be able to survive spiritually in a place where they were steeped in that struggle. And, as we saw above, the struggle of immorality and indulgence was one that was deeply ingrained in the DNA of humanity from the earliest generations of mankind.

THE ORIGINS OF WATERY CORRUPTION

To understand how deeply the corruption of the water element was ingrained in humanity, we need to once again travel back to the early stories of the Torah. After the events of the Garden of Eden and Cain and Abel, which represented the struggle of the earth element, the world didn't get any better!

Over the next ten generations, the world plunged deeper and deeper into immorality. Theft, sexual immorality, and forbidden desires were everywhere one turned. In essence, the traits that are connected to the water element were being corrupted. God decided that all of mankind, except for the righteous Noah and his family, should be destroyed. God destroyed them by bringing a massive flood of water. It was the inner element of water that they had corrupted, so water was the appropriate consequence.

It was the aspect of the corruption and impurity embedded in humanity going back to the generation of the Flood that the Jewish People were meant to refine in Egypt.

In fact, the Sages teach that it was in the merit of the Jewish People creating boundaries, specifically in the area of immorality, that

---

1 The exact time period that the Jewish People were enslaved is a matter of much discussion. A papyrus from the Ramesside Period, dated at approximately in 1150 BCE, depicts many immoral acts done in Egypt.

2 *Rashi, Vayikra* 18:3.

they were redeemed. One of the sages, Rav Huna, adds: "Sarah [the matriarch] went down to Egypt and did not fall prey to immorality; therefore, the Jewish women had the strength to protect themselves. Joseph descended to Egypt and controlled himself from immorality, and in his merit the men had the strength to protect themselves from immorality."[3]

Additionally, our Sages award the bulk of the credit in this area to the women who kept the fire of love and passion burning in their marriages:

> *While the Israelites were making bricks in Egypt, Pharaoh decreed that they were not to sleep at home so that they would not have marital relations with their wives. R. Simeon the son of Halafta said: What did the Israelite women do? They would go to the Nile to draw water, and the Holy One, blessed be He, would fill their jugs with little fishes. They would sell some and cook some, and use some to purchase wine, and then bring it to their husbands in the fields... While the men were eating and drinking, the women would take out their mirrors and glance into them with their husbands. They would say: "I am more attractive than you," and the men would reply: "I am handsomer than you." In that way, they would arose their desires and become fruitful and multiply.*[4]

As is the way of our holy Sages, in telling us an ancient story about life in Egypt, they are also giving us timeless wisdom and advice. The lesson gleaned from this could not be more relevant to our present situation today.

WHEN A PERSON'S MORALE IS LOW, THE TENDENCY IS TO LOOK TOWARD UNHEALTHY AND EVEN FORBIDDEN PLEASURES TO NUMB THE PAIN.

Certainly, the slavery brought down their overall morale. When a person's morale is low, the tendency is to look toward unhealthy and even forbidden

---

3 *Vayikra Rabbah* 32:5.

4 *Midrash Tanchuma, Parshas Pikudei*. See *Sotah* 11b where the Talmud says that it was "in the merit of the righteous women that the Jews were redeemed." The Talmud goes on to give a similar account.

pleasures to numb the pain. We see this in modern times more than ever, especially with men. If he is feeling unfulfilled at work or unsuccessful in his day-to-day activities, inevitably his damaged ego will affect his personal life. Instead of sharing it or discussing it with the people who care about him most, like his wife, he may completely shut her out.

In doing so, he triggers a chain reaction. She feels that there is distance, and without emotional connection, she begins to grow distant and cold as well. Now, his inner pain has been exacerbated, and that vacuum inside him has expanded. Desperate to find some relief and some escape, he may throw himself into all sorts of time-wasting activities, unhealthy pastimes, and even forbidden pleasures. As he engages in these activities, the endorphins that he so badly needs are released in his brain and associate these activities with the only possible way to make him feel whole again. All the while, his closest relationships are suffering.

What our Sages are describing here is how the women understood the nature of men and how they had the ability to give them the emotional strength to withstand Egyptian temptation by infusing their marital life with passion and intimacy. They engaged in this campaign to make their husbands feel desired and vibrant, giving them the fortitude to withstand the other temptations. In this merit, the Jewish People were redeemed. And all of this happened specifically by the water, the symbol of love and affection.

In an environment that capitalized on human lusts and brought out the immoral side of it, the women kept front and center the tremendous holiness that is generated in moments of intimacy between husband and wife. These special mirrors that the women used to adorn themselves would later find a prominent place in the Tabernacle, as we will see later. They would be used in the creation of the washbasin, a symbol of holiness and purity.

But the allusion of the holiness of this intimacy would find an even more prominent place: in the Holy of Holies itself, referred to by our Sages as "the chamber of beds."[5] This further emphasizes that, in

5 II Kings 11:2; *Kinnos* 40.

Judaism, physical intimacy is an incredibly powerful tool to fuse two people together—not just on a physical level, but on an emotional and even spiritual level as well.

SOUL CONNECTIONS

In the last chapter, we saw how there are many soul connections throughout the Torah, and specifically ones that link together the early corrupt generations of humanity and the experience of the Jewish People in Egypt. Returning to the generation of the Flood, the great kabbalistic works teach us a fascinating idea. They explain that the people of that generation actually had unbelievable spiritual potential, so much so that God had, in fact, intended to bestow upon them the ultimate enlightenment by giving them the Torah. But in order to be worthy of receiving the Torah, they would have had to overcome the tremendous temptations that were available to them. Not only did they fail to do so, but they also wound up falling to even deeper levels of impurity.

This Kabbalistic idea brings up one of the most essential lessons in Jewish spirituality and in the struggle to control our temptations: The more spiritual potential that a human being has, the more his soul is also vulnerable to temptation if the spiritual thirst is not quenched. This is because the water element needs to be channeled properly or it can overwhelm a person.

> THE MORE SPIRITUAL POTENTIAL THAT A HUMAN BEING HAS, THE MORE HIS SOUL IS ALSO VULNERABLE TO TEMPTATION IF THE SPIRITUAL THIRST IS NOT QUENCHED.

This incredible principle was eventually discovered in the world of psychology and became the foundational principle behind the famous Twelve-Step program, the world's most successful system of addiction recovery.

The program, founded by a recovering addict named Bill Wilson, was based on a powerful observation from world-renowned psychiatrist Dr. Carl Jung, namely that people with a high level of addiction almost never recover without some sort of "vital spiritual experience." When he heard about the success that addict friends of his had experienced based on this principle, Wilson, who had all but given up hope on himself, adopted a spiritual practice for himself. This helped him recover, and he went on to establish the most powerful program in addiction recovery.

Decades later, Bill Wilson wrote a letter of thanks to Jung. Jung's reply is chilling, as it sheds light not only to the underpinnings of addiction, but the deeply ingrained human craving to connect to spirituality. He writes that "craving for alcohol was the equivalent, on a low level, of the spiritual thirst of our being for wholeness, expressed in medieval language: the union with God."

This generation of the Flood had a spiritual thirst that was meant to be channeled toward the holy ways as the righteous Noah did. Instead, it was channeled toward immorality to the point that God felt that a flood needed to wash them out and cleanse them. But the spiritual DNA of humanity had been affected. Centuries later, when God would be priming the Jewish People to receive the Torah, they would have to descend to an immoral Egypt and show that, unlike that earlier generation, they were strong enough to withstand the temptations.

The soul connection between the generation of the Flood and the Israelites is alluded to strongly in the events that surrounded Moses's birth. Pharaoh had commanded the Egyptians to drown baby Jewish boys in the Nile River. In order to save baby Moses from the Egyptian soldiers, he was placed in a floating box on the river. The Torah refers to the box with the Hebrew word *teivah*, the same word used to describe the ark that saved Noah from the flood. The Hebrew name for Moses is *Moshe*, which comes from the same root as to draw forth, because he was drawn out of the water. But it would also define his life mission—to draw the Jewish People out of the immoral environment of Egypt and elevate the element of water.[6]

---

6 The Talmud (*Chullin*) also points out that Moses's name is hinted to in the Torah's account of the Flood. The weak nature of mankind is attributed to the fact that he is mere flesh, in Hebrew "*b'sha'gam hu basar*." The numerical value of "*b'sha'gam*" equals 345, the same value as the word *Moshe*. And in a later Torah portion, when Moses is defending the Jewish People after the sin of the golden calf, he tells God that if you destroy the Jewish People, "*mecheini*—erase me" from your book. The Hebrew word "*mecheini*" is the very same letters as "*mei Noach*," the waters of Noah.

THE HEALING WATERS OF MIKVAH

Let me now share with you the happy ending of the story that opened this chapter, an ending that will be much more appreciated in light of this new understanding about the element of water.

Feeling that she needed to get away, the embattled wife signed up for an inspirational trip to Israel. The Jewish piece in her life had been missing as well. They were semi-active in their synagogue but didn't have very much Jewish connection in their life, which she hoped she could rekindle on this trip.

A couple of days into the trip, the women took a tour of a beautiful mikvah[7] in the mystical city of Tzefat (Safed).

The guide spoke to the women about the beautiful mitzvah of using the mikvah: how married couples separate from any sort of intimacy and even physical contact for some time, and how the woman then immerses in the mikvah before resuming intimate connection with her spouse. The educator shared several stories of how this mitzvah had revitalized many marriages where the intimacy had faded away and brought about a new sense of love and affection between the couple.

She described both the very practical benefits of separating, but also the mystical significance of immersing in water: how the water element represents desire, but also spiritual connection; how the primordial element of creation is water when there was nothing more than God's desire to bestow His goodness upon another being; and how water represents the source of all life.

Deeply inspired by the experience, the woman decided that, perhaps, this could save her marriage, but was afraid that her husband would never go for it. Already feeling insecure about his lack of ability to keep the passion in his marriage alive, what were the chances that the thought of a Jewish practice being imposed upon him would be something that resonated with him?

---

7 A pool of natural water used for ritual immersion.

After arriving home, she put the idea aside, but it did not stop pulling at her heart. Each time her husband would come home and click on the television, each dinner that they would sit at the table and barely make eye contact, each evening that she would drift off to sleep in her loneliness with only her phone to keep her company, made her yearn more and more for this spiritual revitalization.

Her birthday was coming up, and she made the decision that she could no longer go on like this. She felt that this was the last chance for her marriage. She knew the one thing that her husband always showed up for was her birthday—usually with lavish gifts like jewelry, or even a cruise from time to time. Shortly before her birthday, she wrote him a short note, saying that this year for her birthday, she wanted nothing more than going through the mikvah routine...just this once.

It is hard to know whether it was the mystical power of mikvah or the holiness of this woman, but after those few weeks of physical separation and their reuniting both intimately and emotionally, they both felt that the reset button had been pressed and that the time was right for them to begin the process of healing their marriage, which they slowly did.

As the famous proverb goes: "As a face reflects in water, so does one's heart to another."[8] When we see our reflection in water, we realize that we are looking at ourselves. The inner element of water, our yearning for deep connection, opens us up to see another as a part of us. The closer two human beings are to each other, the greater their emotional states are reflected in each other and affect one another. Her resentment becomes his pain. His distance becomes her emptiness. But when one member of the relationship decides to open up a channel of love toward the other one, that, too, will be reflected in the other, and the loving waters will be reawakened inside them.

THE CLOSER TWO HUMAN BEINGS ARE TO EACH OTHER, THE GREATER THEIR EMOTIONAL STATES ARE REFLECTED IN EACH OTHER AND AFFECT ONE ANOTHER.

8 Proverbs 27:19.

We come to RULE over the water element when we start to recognize and understand that our inner voids are often just a way that our *nefesh* is expressing a deep yearning for real love and connection. With that in mind, we can look at the various relationships in our life and ask ourselves whether we are emotionally present in the way that is necessary for this relationship to thrive. Perhaps the closeness in an important relationship is missing; a spark that was once there has been extinguished. Perhaps we have grown distant with someone who needs us close. But with a little tending to, perhaps that intimacy and passion can be nourished, and the spark reignited. Then, the river of love, pleasure, and connection can flow once again.

summary

- The water element is the source of our desire for pleasure, and it can be channeled toward deep, loving relationships or channeled toward forbidden lust and overindulgence.
- Egypt is deeply connected with the element of water, as they were steeped in immorality. The Jewish women are credited for keeping the morale of the nation alive by keeping the peace and inspiring passion in their marriages.
- The flaw of forbidden lust is rooted in the generation of Noah, which was eventually wiped out by a flood of water.
- The element of water is symbolic of the yearning for deep connection, as we see with the mitzvah of mikvah. Just as water reflects what is close to it, the closer two human beings are to each other, the greater their emotional states are reflected in each other and affect one another.

chapter six

FINDING YOUR VOICE

ELEMENT	THE STRUGGLE	THE ORIGIN
Wind	False beliefs, corrupted speech	The people of Bavel

PRE-CONDITIONING

We move now to the wind element, the inner element connected to our intellect and expressed through our power of speech. As mentioned before, the wind element is connected to the flaw of levity, which includes giving importance to trivialities, making light of serious matters, embracing false beliefs, and the corruption of speech.

Imagine this scene; perhaps you have been here before. You are enjoying the company and the pleasant conversations of family and friends. Everyone is happy and calm. Suddenly, from across the table, someone brings up the latest trending, controversial, hot-button topic. The one that *everyone* is talking about. The one that *everyone* is posting about. The one that inevitably will offend someone. Maybe it's political, religious, or has to do with another emerging social trend. Whatever it is, it gets under your skin whenever you hear about it.

What began as a comment triggered another, and then another, and now, it has fanned into a full-blown heated conversation. The worst thing is that, in this conversation and in this context, you can't even express your opinion. It is one of those issues where the court of mainstream opinion has ruled how you must think, and if you see things differently, you are opening yourself up to a barrage of criticism, name calling, and perhaps even total excommunication. Instead, you must sit quietly, nodding on the outside, while, on the inside, trying to keep your blood pressure in check.

You deeply believe that there are others at the table who probably agree with you, or those who may be open to hearing your perspective. But they are also undercover. How do you find them? How do you connect with them?

There are many people whose opinions are simply formed by whatever is trending at the time. If you are not one of those people, then you have likely experienced the scenario above. Many tyrannic countries throughout history have enforced laws limiting what people can speak about or write about. Our society, which is supposed to celebrate freedom of speech, often feels limiting in that way, as we have established our own cultural rules of what may and may not be spoken about and which viewpoints may or may not be expressed.

This domination of how we are supposed to think and feel is what our Sages refer to as "The Exile of Speech."[1] This can happen because of a tyrannic country, a hostile community, or even within a family or friend circle where the expectation is that everyone will accept the same viewpoints and perspectives. In any place where individuals can't freely express themselves for fear of being demonized, or even if they have no one to share it with, we may say that this person's speech is in exile. And the most tragic example is when people have completely stopped developing their own perspectives, since it is a given how they must think and feel about certain things.

Our thoughts are compared to the wind: having almost no form and mass, always moving, always changing, sometimes stormy, sometimes calm. Like the blowing wind that is an agent for movement, change, and transportation, human beings are meant to use their intellectual power to constantly evolve, grow, and expand. Quite the opposite of the stagnation that is implied in the word *Mitzrayim*, which means trapped or constrained. When we use our intellect to try to discover the ultimate truths, we are elevating the element of wind. When we try

---

1 *Zohar Hakadosh* 25b.

to deepen our understanding of God and the meaning of our existence, refining our values and goals, i.e., what we are living for and who we are meant to be, these are all ways to elevate our intellect. When we pursue Torah study and moral ethics, we are elevating the wind element. It is because of this that wind is associated with *chochmah*, wisdom, as well as curiosity.[2]

We cannot be considered free if we have yet to develop our own unique perceptions and expressions in life. Beliefs based only on what we were conditioned to believe, formed in an environment where we could not really decipher truth from falsehood on our own, reflects the opposite of true freedom. Instead, we must cultivate curiosity and courage to fully explore our convictions, to clarify and to go even deeper into what we believe and why we believe it. Only when a person is actively choosing his belief system can we say that he is truly free.

ONLY WHEN A PERSON IS ACTIVELY CHOOSING HIS BELIEF SYSTEM CAN WE SAY THAT HE IS TRULY FREE.

Egypt is referred to in Kabbalistic texts as "The Exile of Speech" because of how Pharaoh sought to control the thoughts and the speech of the Jewish People. Pharaoh made a mockery of God and shut down any conversation that spoke of God. The most blatant expression of this was when Moses came to Pharaoh with a message from God to release the nation:

> *Afterward, Moses and Aaron went and said to Pharaoh, "Thus says the Lord, the God of Israel: 'Let My people go so that they may celebrate for Me in the wilderness.'" But Pharaoh said, "Who is the Lord that I should heed Him and let Israel go? I do not know the Lord, nor will I let Israel go."*[3]

Pharaoh also tried to stop the Jewish people from thinking about God, by making it as complicated as possible for the Jewish People to complete their projects. By not providing them with bricks and making them scatter across the land to meet their quota, Pharaoh intended that

---

2 Deuteronomy 34:9.

3 Exodus 5:1–2.

not only would it require all their physical effort and time, but their mental effort as well, as they had to figure out ways to meet the demand. It would also separate them from one another as they scattered through the land in search of materials, so that they couldn't engage in meaningful conversation with each other.

The name Pharaoh has the same letters as the word *oref*, which is the nape, the back of the neck. The neck is a place that separates our head from our heart, representing the space between our intellect (what we know) and emotions (what we feel). Our intellect is meant to guide our emotions and our decision making. For a person to truly feel inner freedom, he must have unity between his intellect and his emotional realm. It is the partnership between the wind element (intellect) and water element (emotions) that give birth to holy decisions. When water is introduced in the Torah as the primordial element of creation, it is in tandem with the "wind of the Lord blowing over it."

Imagine a person who is intellectually committed to a certain belief or approach to life but doesn't *feel* comfortable living in that way. If he conforms and lives his life according to what he thinks, despite the emotional disconnect, he will never feel fully free. But if he lives life according to what feels good and neglects what he believes, he won't be any better off. He will constantly feel that cognitive dissonance—feeling that he is not enough. It is only through deep exploration into what he believes and why he believes it that he can develop that emotional piece as well.

Pharaoh's name, which represents the nape, is symbolic of a disconnection between what we know intellectually and what we feel emotionally.

THE POWER OF SPEECH

The wind element is also connected to the power of speech. This is not only because the wind that comes from our vocal cords formulates into the words that we speak (hence, we refer to one who talks a lot as being "long-winded"), but because our words are the vehicle of our intellect, the expression of our thoughts into the world, and they help us concretize what is going on in our brain. Our thoughts are often abstract and hazy, but when we talk something out, it helps us gain clarity on the matter. Speech also helps us calm our train of thought, and many meditations will use a mantra to settle the constant activity of the "monkey mind."

Moreover, words are the building blocks of creation, and refining our speech is considered one of the most important values. God creates the world by speaking it into existence, and when God blows a soul into the first man, our Sages define that moment as the one where man gained his power of speech.[4] Speech is therefore an expression of the soul into this physical world.

WORDS ARE THE BUILDING BLOCKS OF CREATION, AND REFINING OUR SPEECH IS CONSIDERED ONE OF THE MOST IMPORTANT VALUES.

Speaking is not only how we communicate with other human beings, but it is our primary method of connecting Heaven and Earth, the spiritual with the physical. We pray and study Torah using our words and make blessings on all of our worldly pleasures as a means of elevating physical objects and unlocking the spiritual energy that is contained within them.

Therefore, one who cannot express himself because he is unable to do so or because he is not allowed to do so is lacking his freedom and is considered in exile, even if he is in the comfort of his own home.

The great Kabbalist Rabbi Chaim Vital says that gossip, lies, and flattery all fall under the category of the corruption of the wind element.

If we take a look at another permutation of the letters in Pharaoh's name, we see the words *peh ra*, evil speech. We see Pharaoh slandering the Jewish People several times throughout the story. According to the Midrash, Pharaoh was also sly and dishonest as he tried to engage the Jewish nation in a building project that he said would be a joint Egyptian and Jewish project.[5] Slowly but surely, the Egyptians stepped off the project, leaving it solely to the Jewish People.

It is for this reason that we emphasize speech at the Passover Seder when we celebrate our freedom. Our commentaries point out that the

---

4 *Targum Onkelos*, Genesis 2:7.

5 The Torah refers to the hard work as *parech*, which can be broken down to "*b'feh rach*" (with a soft mouth); see *Sotah* 11a–b.

Hebrew word for Passover, *Pesach*, can be broken down into two words "*peh sach*," the mouth that speaks.

THE ORIGINS OF CORRUPT THOUGHT AND SPEECH

As we saw previously, the various elements that were in exile in Egypt all tie back to the early generations of humanity. We have seen how the stories of Cain and Abel and the generation of the Flood were deeply connected to the slavery in Egypt. The next generation in the early stories of humankind—the people of Bavel—once again emerges as a corrupt generation, albeit in a different way from the previous generation of the Flood.

Here, we see a much more sophisticated and intellectual generation, recognized for being united through their power of speech, with the Torah introducing them by telling us that "the entire land was of one language and uniform words." It is this unity of language that would be used to rebel against God, as they devised a very complex plan to distance themselves from God by building "a city and a tower with its top in the heavens." The actual function of this tower is not made clear, but the commentaries understand this to be some form of pagan-worship practice so they could live life as they pleased without any repercussions. Their goal was to devise a system in which they would be able to govern themselves without any Divine intervention, manipulating other heavenly powers.

THE MORE MANKIND DISCOVERS THE INNER WORKINGS OF CREATION, THE MORE THIS INCREASES THE TEMPTATION TO SEE THE WORLD AS RUNNING COMPLETELY INDEPENDENT FROM A DIVINE POWER.

Like some in the modern scientific community, who choose to use their knowledge as an escape from any sort of belief in God, the story of the Tower of Bavel shows that the more mankind discovers the inner workings of creation, the more this increases the temptation to see the world as running completely independent from a Divine power. Rather than using their tremendous wisdom as a means to acknowledge the great wonders that God wove into every aspect of the cosmos, there will be those who will go to great efforts to build "towers" of rationalizations as to why this is not the hand of God (often to the point that it takes even greater "faith" to be an atheist than to be one who believes in God). Their "unity of language" can be understood further as the "groupthink" attitude discussed above, where individuals do not think for themselves but just go along with what is the popular belief of the time.

God does not approve of this behavior and thus responded then by declaring, "Let's confuse their language so that one will not understand the language of his companion." He scattered them like the wind upon the earth, causing the beginnings of the concept of nationhood—diverse nationalities with differing ideals, identifications, and, of course, language. But most significantly, the spiritual DNA of humanity was affected.

The Jewish People in Egypt, in refining themselves to be ready to receive the Torah, must encounter the "exile of speech" and surmount it. The verses themselves use very specific language to provide subtle hints to the connection between the Tower of Bavel and Egypt,[6] as we will see shortly.

SOUL CONNECTIONS

Just as we saw with the generation of the Flood, here too, the Kabbalists teach about a deep soul connection between this early generation and the Jewish People in Egypt. The people of Bavel, like the generation of the Flood, also had the ability to receive the Torah and become a spiritually enlightened generation. Instead, they corrupted their ways by turning to paganism and swapping belief in one true God for the "mortar and bricks."

The Torah calls our attention to the link between these two generations by describing the Jewish People's hard work of building with "mortar and bricks," the only other time in the Torah that this exact language is used! Eventually, the Egyptians intensified the Jewish People's

---

6 The very same language that the people of Bavel used to unify together—"Come, let us build us a city, and a tower with its top in the sky, to make a name for ourselves; or else we shall be scattered all over the world"—is mirrored by the Egyptians who declare, "Come, let us deal shrewdly with them, so that they may not increase; or else in the event of war they may join our enemies in fighting against us and rise from the ground." This specific choice of words is only found in these two places in the Torah.

slavery by ceasing to supply them with bricks and requiring them to meet the quota nonetheless. The Torah describes the scene as "then the people scattered throughout the land of Egypt to gather stubble for straw."[7] This, again, parallels the language used when God disrupted the plan of the architects of the tower: "Thus Hashem scattered them from there over the face of the whole earth; and they stopped building the city."[8]

On a deeper level, the Torah is teaching us that the Jewish People were engaged in a process of refining the corruption of thought and speech that was the hallmark of the generation of the Tower of Bavel. Their inability to speak freely with one another and to commune together for holy purposes would make them truly value one another and appreciate the power of community. In contradistinction to the generation of the Tower of Bavel, which exemplified the dangers of groupthink and had to be dispersed because of their negative influences upon each other, the Jewish People would experience the reverse of that, as the redemption would ultimately lead them to the greatest experience of unity when they would stand around Mount Sinai "as one man with one heart."

And, in contrast to the generation of the Tower of Bavel, where the Torah says that God "descended to look at the city and tower" in disapproval, at Mount Sinai, the Torah tells us, "God descended upon the Mountain." This time, however, it was to crown the Jewish People with the gift of brotherhood and nationhood, and to reveal to them the ultimate truths of existence in the form of the Ten Commandments.

In Hebrew, the ten "commandments" are referred to as the *Aseres Hadibros*, which is most accurately translated as the ten statements. This will be a symbol of the fact that, at that point, true freedom of the power of speech had been achieved. And who better to deliver that message than Moses, the one who began the story as being unable to speak. Standing on the mountain, though, the Torah proclaims, "Moses speaks and God echoes with a voice."[9]

---

7 Exodus 5:12.

8 Genesis 11:8.

9 Exodus 19:19.

In our own lives, we come to RULE over our wind element when we learn to how to properly use our power of intellect and power of speech. This happens when we learn to think for ourselves and investigate deeply the things that we believe—rather than just going along with the crowd—when we feel that we are safe to engage in meaningful conversations, to ask questions, and to share our opinions.

The first step to doing so is asking ourselves what the source of our beliefs and information really is. Ancient texts, spiritual teachers, and people who we deeply respect will all guide us to clarity of thinking and meaningful conversations. Prayer and meditation will give us clarity of mind to see the world from an elevated place. In contrast to this, agenda-driven media, social media, leaders whose motives are questionable, and those who engage in gossip and nasty speech will lead us down the same road as the people of Bavel and will eventually result in a fragmented and polarized world.

summary

- The wind element is about intellect and speech, and is only considered free when they can honestly explore and express their beliefs.
- Egypt is referred to as the Exile of Speech because it did not allow the Jewish People to remain connected to their faith or engage in holy pursuits like prayer and meaningful conversation.
- Flawed speech and intellect are rooted in the generation that caused the Tower of Bavel. The corruption of that generation was also born out of the pressure of groupthink and persuasion toward a false belief system.
- In order to elevate the element of wind, we must learn to think for ourselves and investigate deeply the things that we believe, rather than just going along with the crowd. We need to feel that we are safe to engage in meaningful conversations, to ask questions, and to share our opinions.

chapter seven

THE EGO AND OTHER SHINY OBJECTS

ELEMENT	THE STRUGGLE	THE ORIGIN
Fire	Arrogance, obsession with materialism	The city of Sodom

WHAT SUCCESS LOOKS LIKE

You made it big. Maybe you scored the corner office, or you take trips to exotic locations on the corporate jet. You've got the designer shoes, dine at the highest-end restaurants, and sit in the luxury suites. All of this indicates that you have hit the success metrics. But they certainly don't seem to be a good recipe for humility. Perhaps, this is why people who make it high on the corporate ladder are often stereotyped as being conceited and egocentric. But that certainly isn't always the case.

Our discussion now moves to the fire element, the inner element connected to our will and self-esteem. The fire element is connected to our ego and can lead a person to arrogance and too much preoccupation with oneself.

The fire element inside of us is the part of us that needs to feel a sense of worth, to know that we matter. In order to do this, we are consciously or subconsciously searching for ways to define ourselves and to give ourselves the feeling that we are accomplishing. If it is our higher consciousness directing our search, we will look for what is authentic and true and right for us. If not, then we can fall into the trap of defining ourselves by what society calls success and spend a lifetime trying to live up to those metrics, no matter how superficial they may be.

As writer Eckhart Tolle says:

> *One of the most basic levels of identification is with things: my toy later becomes my car, my house, my clothes, and so on. I try to find myself in things but never quite make it and end up losing myself in them. That is the fate of the ego...When you can no longer feel the life that you are, you are likely to try to fill up your life with things.*

As we mentioned earlier, any force inside of us that blurs our ability to make the best possible decisions is essentially an inner Pharaoh. Our egos make many decisions for us all the time. It gets really noisy when we are buying a new car or looking to purchase a new home or when we are going clothes shopping and, for some, even when they are looking for a marriage partner. It is really busy at social gatherings and networking events as we try to work the crowd and pepper our conversations with subtle self-promotion, humble-bragging, and name dropping. And when we start experiencing some sort of success and abundance, the ego is quick to fill us up with pride and tell us that we are better than others.

OUR EGOS MAKE MANY DECISIONS FOR US ALL THE TIME.

But many successful yet humble people see their success as a gift from Above, a reason to be grateful, and a charge to take on more responsibility for others and for the world. They allow themselves to experience the sense of accomplishment for all the effort, energy, and diligence that it takes to achieve success, while never losing focus that much of it is out of our hands and comes from Above. This includes the intelligence that was the gift of our genetic makeup, the connections that could have easily not happened, the timing that just worked out in our favor, and, let's not forget, that little bit of "luck" (or as Jewish tradition more accurately calls it, a little bit of *mazal*). As Warren Buffet, the great investor, points out, "The womb from which you emerge determines your fate to an enormous degree for most of the seven billion people in the world."

The opposite attitude of this is what is commonly referred to as "self-attribution bias." Self-attribution bias is the tendency to dismiss the situational reasons that may have caused something to happen and instead see it as a reflection of the person. So, if someone cuts you off while driving, for example, the person is certainly a jerk or a bad driver. But if you were that person who had done the cutting off, you would rationalize that you were confused by the unclear directions that Siri or Waze gave you. And when there is self-attribution bias, we may be quick to take full credit when things go right, but just as quickly attribute our failures to situational factors. This mode of thinking is a by-product of our ego or, as we refer to it here, our inner Pharaoh.

Pharaoh is the archetype for the egocentric success story and the inner voice of arrogance, who attributes everything to himself and nothing to God. He is the textbook narcissist. This is why Pharaoh is described as the "Mighty sea monster, sprawling in your channels, who said, 'My Nile is my own, and I created myself.'"[1]

Egypt sits along the Nile River, which would regularly overflow its banks and irrigate the land. This created a dependable water-source, as opposed to the other lands of the region, such as Israel, which heavily depends on rain for its water. This allowed Egypt to amass its famous power, wealth, and military capability that most other nations in the area did not have. This led the Egyptians, and especially Pharaoh, to feel completely secure and completely independent of God.

The Egyptians came to worship the Nile, represented by the Egyptian God referred to as Sobek, with the head of a crocodile and green skin. (If you have ever gone to the Smithsonian National History Museum, you might notice the Egyptian fascination with the crocodile.) The "mighty monster" referred to in the verse above is *tanin* in Hebrew, translated by many commentaries as a crocodile. The verse above is describing how Pharaoh viewed himself as an embodiment of the god of the Nile, believing that he could take credit for all of Egypt's success. Self-attribution bias to the extreme.

---

1 Ezekiel 29:3.

The ego can make a person forget about God completely or create a false sense that he is somehow equal with God. In the recovery program Alcoholics Anonymous, it's taught that ego stands for Easing God Out. This leads to arrogance and even narcissism, and it can bring out the most monstrous aspects of a human being.

But channeled properly, the element of fire can create an awareness inside of a person of his innate greatness. He isn't God, but he has a spark of Godliness inside of him, and therefore, he has the potential to manifest that Godliness in his life. We see this in the fact that the very first human being was named Adam. This name comes from the word *adameh*, which means "I am similar," a reference to the fact that every single human being is similar to God, as each is created in the image of God. But this very same word is also similar to *adamah*, earth, reminding a person to not forget his place, i.e., where he comes from.

THE ORIGIN OF FIERY NARCISSISM

Rewinding back to the early stories of the Torah, we can see the flaw of fire in the next major tragedy in the story of humanity. We have seen how the story of Cain corresponds to earth, how the flood connects to the water element, and how the people of Bavel were rooted in the wind element. Shortly after, we are introduced to two extremely affluent cities, Sodom and Gomorrah, which are infamous for their evil ways, their arrogance, and their inhospitality. If you weren't part of their clubs and cliques, you were completely rejected for being inferior to them.[2] They are therefore synonymous with greed, inhospitality, and indulgence in the material way of life, all of which are associated with the element of fire. Their behavior would be the equivalent of modern-day communities whose affluence has driven them to the point where individuals are measured by their net worth, the size of their house, what car they drive,

2 The Torah refers to the sin of Sodom as "heavy" (Genesis 18:20). The word heavy in Hebrew, *kaveid*, has the same letters as the Hebrew word for honor, *kavod*. This is echoed by the great prophet Ezekiel: "Only this was the sin of your sister Sodom: arrogance! She and her daughters had plenty of bread and untroubled tranquility; yet she did not support the poor and the needy. In their haughtiness, they committed abomination before Me; and so I removed them, as you saw" (Ezekiel 16:49).

and what brands they are wearing. The consequence of the narcissism of Sodom and Gomorrah was their destruction by a storm of fire.

Additionally, the Torah notes that the remnants of Sodom were like salt. The city of Sodom was located near the Dead Sea, known for its high concentration of salts. In ancient times, salt was an important commodity not only because of its role in flavor enhancement, but because of its crucial role in preserving foods (in a time before refrigerators), and its medicinal properties. Salt was often used as currency to such an extent that the root of the word "salary" is the Latin word *sal*, meaning salt.[3]

Sodom's proximity to the Dead Sea and the Jordan River may have been one of the sources of its wealth and the cause of its influence. Therefore, their destruction came about measure for measure, as the verse states: "Brimstone and salt burned the entire land so that nothing could be grown, nor any grass arise, like the overturning of Sodom."[4] The very symbol of its wealth was made into the symbol of its destruction.

One sees many similarities to Sodom and Egypt. They were both wealthy because of their location, a factor outside of their control, yet they allowed it to get to their head and swell their egos. The Torah seems to hint to this similarity when describing the abundance of Sodom using the description: "like the garden of the Lord, like the land of Egypt."[5]

INSTEAD OF THE ABUNDANCE BRINGING BLESSING, IT OFTEN LEAVES TRAGEDY IN ITS WAKE: SCARRED RELATIONSHIPS, DEPRESSION, AND ANXIETY.

And in both of those cases, their abundance ultimately leads to their downfall. This is tragically similar to what we see today when a society becomes too occupied with status symbols and vanity metrics. Instead of the abundance bringing blessing, it often leaves tragedy in its wake: scarred relationships, depression, and anxiety. And the frightening thing is that this preoccupation spreads

---

3 Efraim Palvanov, *Secrets of the Last Waters* (Lulu.com, April 2014).

4 Deuteronomy 29:22.

5 Genesis 13:10.

quickly in communities and can be as hard to control as a bad virus. In fact, a term that was popularized over the past few decades perfectly illustrates the virus-like symptoms of the dangers of affluence. The term is "affluenza," and it can be defined as "a painful, contagious, socially transmitted condition of overload, debt, anxiety, and waste resulting from the dogged pursuit of more." As British psychologist Dr. Oliver James describes it:

> *The Affluenza Virus is a set of values which increase our vulnerability to emotional distress. It entails placing a high value on acquiring money and possessions, looking good in the eyes of others and wanting to be famous.*

According to Kabbalah, whether a person's wealth will bring with it blessing or destruction is actually dependent on what the heavenly source of the abundance is. In other words, not all wealth flows from the same place. When a person receives heavenly abundance when he is in a state of humility and gratitude, he receives it from a heavenly source metaphorically referred to as God's *panim*, or face/front. But if it is received by a person who is in a state of ego and entitlement, it descends from a heavenly source referred to as God's *oref*, or nape/back.[6] This is the secret as to why some individuals can have less but find themselves having so much satisfaction; it is because they have received their sustenance from the *panim* of God.

Metaphorically, sustenance coming from heaven can be compared to one who gives charity, which can be done in one of two ways. The giver can look the one who is collecting in the eyes, trying to connect deeply

---

6 In *Festivals of Freedom*, Rav Soloveitchik explains that sustenance that enters the world through *hashpaas panim* goes through a very rigorous filtration process as it flows through the heavenly pipelines, known in Kabbalah as the *Sefiros*. The *Sefiros* are a system where Divine energy and flow begins with total abundance, but slowly constricts and balances itself based on the vessel into which it is flowing, namely how deserving the individual is to receive this blessing. But if all flow would come through this system, we would find a world where the righteous prosper and the evil suffer. This would create an imbalance of free will. So, God unlocks the *hashpaas oref*, allowing it to pour into the world and enter into people's lives by a much more natural means.

with him and what his needs are, and give to him with a smile. He might take the time to fully understand what the recipient's needs are and adjust his gift accordingly. Or he can feel annoyed that he is being asked and throw some charity at the one who is collecting without offering any eye contact or any connection, but, instead, making the collector feel even worse about himself.

If you recall, we mentioned above that the name *Pharaoh* has in it the same letters as the word *oref*, nape. In this context, this symbolizes that all of the heavenly abundance that came upon Egypt came with a cost and, ultimately, led to its destruction.

The ultimate purpose, therefore, of exposing the Jewish People to the Egyptian mindset would be to challenge them to extricate themselves and reject it. Because of their exposure to the Egyptian attitude, the Jews would truly have to appreciate the spiritual challenges of wealth and overcome them. After experiencing how material overload can threaten their connection with God, it would lead them to prioritize spirituality over wealth. As the Chassidic master, Rabbi Natan of Breslov, says: "Israel was exiled to Egypt in order to purify the wealth from there."

It is because of this that our redemption had to come about through Moses, who the Torah describes as the humblest of men despite his wealth and stature. In order to find that personal redemption in our life, the trait of humility is one that we need to cultivate and develop, no matter how high we climb in our own wealth and stature.

SOUL CONNECTIONS

The Midrash teaches that during the plague of darkness, many Jews, who were too embedded in Egyptian culture and would have refused to leave, suffered a plague of their own and died during that time. The Kabbalists suggest further that their punishment coming during the plague of darkness is an allusion to the fact that there was a soul connection to the generation of Sodom, who also suffered blindness before they were destroyed.

Sight is dependent on light, as the light from the object we are looking at moves through space until it reaches our eyes, providing the stimulus for our brain to decipher the appearance and location of the object.

Light itself is associated with the elements of fire. These souls had abused their inner element of fire and refused to see their own true worth and were, therefore, punished with blindness. The Jewish People who refused to leave were too attached to the materialistic way of life, and therefore died during the plague of darkness.

WE ARE AWARE OF THE CURSE OF THE "GOLDEN HANDCUFFS" THAT CHAIN A PERSON TO A TOXIC SITUATION BECAUSE OF THE FINANCIAL SECURITY THAT IT AFFORDS.

It is hard to imagine that there would have been any Jew who didn't want to leave. Yet, we are aware of the curse of the "golden handcuffs" that chain a person to a toxic situation because of the financial security that it affords.

When the family of Jacob first came down to Egypt, they benefited from the tremendous abundance that Egypt had to offer. As a family of the viceroy, they were certainly invited to partake in all the benefits of Egyptian culture. From the onset, they were surrounded by the wealth and splendor of Pharaoh. It was there that they became a people. Egypt welcomed them, and they made themselves at home, to the point that when it came time to leave many Jews did not want to leave the riches of Egypt. Even later on, in the desert after the Exodus, when things would get tough, Jews would reminisce about the lavish lifestyle that they had early on in Egypt. Little did they realize that their comfort in Egypt was leading them to become entrapped and enslaved in those golden handcuffs.

This sends a powerful message through time to all of the descendants of those Jews in Egypt who find prosperity in the various host countries that we find ourselves. The comfort provided by our hosts can often lull us into feeling a little too comfortable and letting go of our identity.

The story is told of the Chassidic master, Reb Menachem Nachum of Chernobyl,[7] who would wake up every night at midnight to mourn the destruction of the Temple. Once, when the Rebbe was staying over at an inn, the owner of the inn awoke

7 The *Meor Einayim* (1770–1837).

to hear the Rebbe's midnight moaning and prayers. He quickly ran to his room to see if everything was OK.

Rav Menachem Nachum apologized and explained to the innkeeper, a simple Jew, about the destruction of the Temple and what it meant, as well as the importance of always yearning for redemption and to return to Israel. Soon the innkeeper was crying as well. Reb Menachem Nachum consoled him by telling him that there will be a redemption very soon, and we will all have the opportunity to return to Israel. He then asked the innkeeper a powerful question, one that Diaspora Jews need to ask themselves frequently: "When it happens, when the redemption comes, will you be ready?"

This was a lot for the innkeeper to process. With much on his mind, he went back to bed but could not sleep. The question circled in his head again and again. With all of his twisting and turning, his wife woke up and inquired why he couldn't sleep. He told her about the Temple, about how in the future the redemption will come, and about how the Jewish People will return to Israel. And then he asked her what the Rebbe asked him: "Will we be ready?"

The innkeeper's wife was a very practical woman and firmly responded, "We absolutely cannot go! We have invested our whole life into this inn and our livestock. We can't just upend our whole life and lose everything!"

Now, the innkeeper really couldn't sleep. He returned to the Rebbe's quarters and told him his wife's response. The Rebbe responded, "My dear friend, why do you feel so secure here in Poland? There is so much anti-Semitism. At any moment, the Tartars and the Cossacks could come and take everything away from you and even kill you. Wouldn't you feel safer if you were in the land of Israel, protected by the Almighty and his promise to the Jewish People?"

This made a deep impact on the innkeeper, who returned to his room. Once again, his wife awoke and the innkeeper reported back what the Rebbe had said. With both of them now deeply seeing the truth in the Rebbe words, they talked and talked until they felt that they came to a solution.

The innkeeper returned to the Rebbe's quarters once again to report back what he and his wife decided. "Rebbe, we discussed it, and my wife came up with the perfect solution. When it is time for the redemption, let's send the Tartars, the Cossacks, and the anti-Semites to the land of Israel, and then we'll be able to stay here peacefully with our beautiful inn and our livestock!"

This humorous story has many layers of truth. Throughout our two-thousand-year exile, the Jewish People have experienced both tremendous poverty and tremendous wealth in various host countries. We have engaged in trade, commerce, and entrepreneurial activities; been moneylenders, bankers, and financiers; had careers in finance, law, medicine, and scholarship. At times, when we are in our lower states, we are very much aware that these host countries aren't where we are supposed to be. But, when we are successful, we tend to get very comfortable, a little too comfortable. Our host countries can often make us forget that we are always supposed to view ourselves as guests while there and only consider the land of Israel our true homeland.

THE ULTIMATE SLAVERY IS NOT CHAINS AND FORCED LABOR BUT THE DEIFICATION OF WEALTH AND HUMAN ACHIEVEMENT.

While we would have assumed that the Jewish People would have been thrilled to leave Egypt, getting them on board wasn't as simple as one would have imagined. In fact, the Jewish People completely rejected Moses, just as he had anticipated! As the old Chassidic saying mentioned earlier goes, "The real exile of Israel in Egypt was that they learned to endure it."

And yet, we celebrate the Exodus from Egypt every year at Passover as if we were free, without even realizing that the ultimate slavery is not chains and forced labor but the deification of wealth and human achievement. All of Egypt was enslaved to perverse materialism, and it was for this reason that God decimated the land and sent Israel out with its wealth.

In order to RULE over the potential pitfalls of the element of fire, we can never feel too attached to our material possessions or superficial identifications. We must search for the things that we truly value about ourselves that are independent of anything that can be lost or taken away, feeling confident and secure, and seeing the inherent greatness in ourselves and in others.

summary

- The fire element is connected to our ego and can lead a person to arrogance and too much preoccupation with oneself. This is because it is the part of us that needs to feel a sense of worth—to know that we matter.
- Egypt sits along the Nile River, which would regularly overflow its banks and irrigate the land. This allowed Egypt to amass its famous power, wealth, and military capability that most other nations in the area did not have. This led the Egyptians, and especially Pharaoh, to feel completely secure and completely independent of God.
- The flaws of the element of fire are rooted in Sodom and Gomorrah, which are infamous for their evil ways, their arrogance, and their inhospitality. They are therefore synonymous with greed, inhospitality, and indulgence in the material way of life, all of which are associated with the element of fire.
- The Jewish nation themselves have always had to face the test of whether we would become too attracted to the materialism of the guest countries that we find ourselves in. In our personal lives as well, we are often tested whether we will become trapped by golden handcuffs, i.e., the lure of materialism.

chapter eight

THE DEEPER MESSAGE OF THE TEN PLAGUES

THE PURPOSE OF THE PLAGUES

In the 1950s, Dr. Curt Richter, a professor at Johns Hopkins University, conducted a powerful (and somewhat cruel) experiment to show the power of hope and resilience. He placed a cohort of similar rats in a pool of water and observed how long they would tread water until they gave up and started to drown. But right before they gave up and started to go under, he would rescue them, allow them to rest for a few minutes, and assist them in recovering.

He then put them back in for a second round, starting the experiment all over again. Incredibly, on the second round, the rats swam and swam for a much longer time than they had done the first time around! The only thing that had changed was that since they had been saved previously, they had more hope this time that they would once again be saved. The conclusion drawn was that with hope that there is a way out, they could push their bodies way past what they previously thought impossible. Curt wrote that "the rats quickly learn that the situation is not actually hopeless" and that "after elimination of hopelessness the rats do not die."

THE POWER OF HOPE CAN PROPEL US TO PUSH OURSELVES WAY PAST WHAT WE PREVIOUSLY THOUGHT WAS IMPOSSIBLE.

This is a powerful lesson not only for rats, but for their application to human psychology as well. The power of hope can propel us to push ourselves way past what we previously thought was impossible.

After over two centuries in Egypt, the Jewish People were drowning. They were on the lowest levels of spiritual impurity and had lost hope. "And the people were not able to listen to Moses because of their shortness of breath." The Jewish People had been abused physically and spiritually and had given up on themselves. It would take something powerful to show them that transformation is always possible.

After an initial failed attempt by Moses to persuade Pharaoh to let the Jewish People go free, which only aggravated the situation, Moses returned to God and pleaded: "O Lord, why did You bring harm upon this people? Why did You send me? Ever since I came to Pharaoh to speak in Your name, he has dealt worse with this people; and still You have not delivered Your people."

At this point, God responds with the four statements of redemption, which, as we mentioned above, are the basis for the four cups of wine: "I will take you out...I will save you...I will redeem you...I will take you to me as a nation."

We now understand the true depth of these words and the significance of the number four. It would take a lot to wake up the Jewish People. The message here was that despite the fact that the Jewish People were enslaved in Egypt and a deep contamination of the four elements, God would extract them step-by-step, element-by-element, until they could experience true freedom—their greatest possible selves.

Additionally, God wasn't just referencing *what* they will be freed from but *how* they will be freed. The entire redemption process will revolve around the four elements, beginning with the ten plagues which, as will see shortly, are deeply connected to the four elements.

The purpose of the ten plagues was not merely to try to compel Pharaoh to send out the Jewish People or to punish the Egyptians, as is so often depicted. The plagues were much more than that. Each plague drove home a powerful message about the power of transformation, specifically in the realm of the four elements. The Jewish People would witness the four elements of the physical world now be transformed into a tool in God's hand to bring about redemption. On an inner level, the four elements that had spiritually enslaved the Jewish People, driving them to reach the lowest spiritual levels, would now be transformed into tools to worship God.

SACRED PATTERNS AND NUMBERS

God specifically sent ten plagues, as the number ten in Kabbalah represents completeness. When God speaks, it usually follows a pattern of ten. For example, our Sages teach that "with ten utterances was the world created," and, at the Jewish People's inauguration into nationhood, God speaks the Ten Commandments at Mount Sinai.

The message of the ten plagues follows this pattern. From the time that God had created the world using the ten utterances until this point, mankind had collectively failed miserably in turning the physical world into a place where God can call His home. With the exception of the patriarchs, the matriarchs, and their children, civilization was full of corruption, idol worship, and depravity—with Egypt as the world leader in all of this—causing God's presence to distance itself and weaken. With the ten plagues, all of this would change. A new surge of Godly current would pulse into creation. It would elevate those who would be willing to become vessels for that Divine light and tear down those who would stand in its way.

The Torah separates the plagues into two groups by placing them in two different Torah portions. The first group consists of the first seven plagues. The second group consists of the final three. This division of seven and three follows a pattern that we see in the other instances of ten in the Torah:

- In the Creation story, God creates the world using ten utterances, yet there are seven days of Creation. Three of the other utterances are hidden within the other days.
- In the giving of the Ten Commandments, we find that seven of them are written as prohibitions (do not murder, commit adultery, steal, etc.), while only three (believing in God, observing the Shabbat, and honoring one's parents) are written as positive commandments.

This pattern can be explained by the Kabalistic principle that the number seven represents completion in the natural order of the physical world and the more tangible aspects in our life. This is why our physical world seems to follow a pattern of seven. The number seven is the number that represents the natural order of the world: There are seven colors in the rainbow, seven musical notes, seven days of the week, seven continents, seven sections of the human body, and seven orifices in our face.

In the Creation story, seven utterances are manifest as units of time that will carry that energy into the world. The other three are hidden in the backdrop. In the Ten Commandments, seven are prohibitions that relate to the areas of life that humanity will struggle, while three relate to pure unadulterated connection with something grander.[1]

This explains the pattern of the plagues as well. The first seven plagues contain all four elements. After those seven plagues, there was a complete revelation that God is in control of all the elements.

In fact, we actually see all four elements represented in the first six. The seventh plague, hail, is actually a combination of all four elements, as it is the "grand finale" of the first group. This is why the seventh plague is introduced with God declaring: "This time I will send **all My plagues** upon you."[2]

The final three plagues moved beyond the four elements and related to the heavenly realm that is beyond matter.

We can see the connection between the first group of plagues and the four elements as follows:

- Blood (#1) and Frogs (#2)—Water Element
- Lice (#3) and Mixed Creatures (#4)—Earth Element
- Pestilence (#5)—Wind Element
- Boils (#6)—Fire Element
- Hail (#7)—all four elements

1 In Kabbalah, Divine energy enters into the world through channels called *Sefiros*. There are ten *Sefiros*, each one representing a different attribute through which the world exists and functions. The *Sefiros* themselves are divided into the groups of seven and three. Three of them are referred to as the revelation of God's "intellect," which express themselves in much more concealed ways. Seven of them are referred to as character traits, and their expression is more tangible in our lives and revealed through world events.

2 Exodus 9:14.

THE PLAGUES

BLOOD AND FROGS: THE WATER ELEMENT

The first two plagues related to the element of water and the flaw of mischanneled lust. In the first plague, all the water turned to blood, representing how when our passion is used the wrong way, it leads to pain and sin. According to the Midrash, the plague of blood paralleled the crime of the Egyptians of closing off the *mikvaos* (ritual baths) of the Jewish People. These were the waters that brought renewal to the intimacy of family life.

This message was deepened with the second plague, with frogs and possibly other amphibious creatures pouring onto the land, inhabiting the Egyptians homes and attacking their bodies. Frogs lived in the Nile in multitudes, so their identity was connected very much to this body of water, which was a life source for the Egyptian people. The frogs' association with the Nile, plus their fertility, led the Egyptians to view them as a symbol for the source of life, and therefore, they treated them as a deity. The Egyptian goddess of fertility was depicted as a frog or a woman with a frog head. The frog was a symbol of fertility, and their images were used to protect pregnant women.

The Torah teaches explicitly that the frogs entered the ovens and their beds, two locations where different types of physical pleasure happen.[3] Furthermore, the Midrash teaches that the frogs castrated the Egyptians.[4]

By turning the Nile and the frogs against the Egyptians, God was sending a message that when the element of water, the power of pleasure, is abused, it becomes a dangerous weapon that can cause much harm.

LICE AND MIXED CREATURES: THE EARTH ELEMENT

The next two plagues were connected to the earth element. The third plague, swarms of lice, emerged "from the dust of the earth." The fourth plague involved mixed creatures (the Sages debate if they were animals

---

3 "The Nile shall swarm with frogs, and they shall come up and enter your palace, your bedchamber and your bed, the houses of your courtiers and your people, and your ovens and your kneading bowls" (Exodus 7:28).

4 *Midrash Rabbah* 15:27.

or insects) who left their habitat and "filled the houses of the Egyptians, and the very ground they stand on."[5]

To fully understand the message of these plagues, we need to remind ourselves of the description of the creation of man all the way back in the Book of Genesis. Man was created on the sixth day of Creation, a day that started off with God proclaiming, "Let the earth bring forth every kind of living creature: cattle, creeping things, and wild beasts of every kind." A bit later in the day the Torah teaches, "God formed man *from the dust of the earth*." We see a very close association between man and animals/creeping things, in that they are both created on the same day and are associated with the element of earth.

However, Jewish tradition teaches that while the physical and biological aspects of man are associated with the earth element, man's soul was actually the first thing created and is of the highest on the spiritual totem pole.

The third and fourth plagues were both reminders that when man corrupts his inner earth element, he has disconnected from his soul and is now on par with the insects and animals that were created on the same day as him. As he was created later on that day, he now becomes powerless against them. The very earth will overpower him, as well as the other creatures that were created before him, and view him as inferior to them.

PESTILENCE: THE WIND ELEMENT

The plagues now move into the realm of wind and the intellect. Our Sages teach that the plague of pestilence came about through a disease that polluted the air (connected to the wind element), causing the Egyptian cattle to die.

The Egyptians worshiped their cattle, viewing them as a symbol of various gods. The female god who they viewed as the mother of the Pharaohs was depicted as a cow and was considered the god of the skies (connected to the wind element). Several other Egyptian gods were also depicted as cattle (either cows or rams, etc.). Therefore, striking

---

5 Exodus 8:17.

the cattle by a disease in the air, carried in by the wind, drove home a powerful rebuke about the corruption of the wind element.

The plague of pestilence is introduced by the Torah in the following way: "Then the hand of God is upon your livestock in the fields—the horses, the asses, the camels, the cattle, and the sheep—with a very severe pestilence."

There is tremendous significance to this plague's association with the "hand of God." Clearly, this was a massive blow to the Egyptians. But what is even more interesting is the strange language that the Torah uses by saying that the hand of God "is upon your livestock," in the present tense. The Hebrew word for "is" in this context is the word *hoyah*, spelled הויה. These are the same letters that spell *Havayah*, a reference to the name of the Almighty that shows His ever-presence and guidance at every moment. It was specifically that name of God that Pharaoh mocked in his original encounter with Moses.

The attack on these powerful Egyptian gods drove home a powerful message about the hand of God, which Pharaoh mocked, and His presence in the day-to-day ongoing of the world. The name *Havayah* was restored.

A final connection can be seen in the Hebrew name of the plague, *dever*, which also shares the same root as *dibbur*, which means speech. We mentioned how the wind element also relates to the corruption of speech. It is the word of God that sustains the world at every moment, constantly powering it into existence.

BOILS: THE FIRE ELEMENT

The connection between the plague of boils and the fire element is first demonstrated in how the plague was brought about:

> *Then Hashem said to Moses and Aaron, "Each of you take handfuls of soot from the kiln, and let Moses throw it toward the sky in the sight of Pharaoh. It shall become a fine dust all over the land of Egypt, and cause an inflammation breaking out in boils on man and beast throughout the land of Egypt."*[6]

---

6 Exodus 9:8–9.

The ashes and the dust from the furnace are, perhaps, the lowest form of the fire elements, nothing more than an unwanted by-product or wasteful content that comes from the fire. It would be this soot that would bring about the downfall of Egypt's most arrogant members, the magicians: "The magicians were unable to confront Moses because of the inflammation, for the inflammation afflicted the magicians as well as all the other Egyptians."[7] The magicians were considered the most brilliant of people in Egypt, the equivalent of the great scientists and doctors of nowadays. The ability to heal another human being is certainly a great gift to humanity, an almost Godly quality, and one can imagine how this feeling of power can certainly go to someone's head. The Egyptian healers were of the greatest deniers of God. They were embarrassed to admit that they had no means to cure this unusual disease. This plague signified how even those who seem infallible can be brought down in a moment, revealing the fickleness of their power and fame.

HAIL: THE FOUR ELEMENTS COMBINED

We mentioned above that the number seven throughout the Torah represents the wholeness of the natural world. Therefore, the seventh plague would be the final one in the first group of plagues and would bring together all four elements in a massive display of God's power in the world, preceded by the declaration by God: "This time I will send **all My plagues**."[8] This miraculous hail would be fire mixed with ice (fire and water element) falling from the heavens (wind element) and bringing destruction to the earth.[9]

After showing the Egyptians through the previous plagues that there was a heavenly hand in each of the elements, this plague would show how all of those four elements could be unified and coordinated to do the will of God. They are not separate powers, but work in tandem with one another.

---

7 Ibid., v. 11.
8 Ibid., v. 14.
9 Ibid., 9:23–25.

The plague of hail is a reminder to us that the elements do not operate in a vacuum. They are often connected. When we allow ourselves to fall in any one area, it is almost certain that we will see struggles in some of the other areas as well.

With the plague of hail, the first group of plagues were complete. At this point, the Jewish People started getting the message: The four elements can either be used as a tool for Godliness or a tool for corruption.

LOCUSTS: ATTRACTING ABUNDANCE

The final three plagues—locusts, darkness, and death of the first-born—would contain their own set of messages about the nature of the soul as being a tool in the hand of God. The final three emanated from a realm above the four elements and represented the true spiritual greatness that the Jewish People would receive as they became a holy nation.

In introducing the plague of locusts, Moses and Aaron deliver the following message:

> *Thus says the Lord, the God of the Hebrews, "How long will you refuse to humble yourself before Me? Let My people go that they may worship Me. For if you refuse to let My people go, tomorrow I will bring arbeh [locusts] on your territory. They shall cover the surface of the land, so that no one will be able to see the land."*[10]

The Hebrew word for locusts is *arbeh*, which comes from the root of multitudes or abundance. The *arbeh* would descend from heaven in such amazing swarms that they would completely cover Egypt making it virtually disappear. The Midrash compares them to an army that invades a city after weeks of siege where it has been weakened.

Our inner world attracts our life circumstances. When we elevate the inner world of the four elements, we will attract abundance and blessings in our life. When we corrupt the four elements, we attract

---

10 Ibid., 10:5.

an abundance of problems until we can no longer see the blessings anymore in our life.

After Adam and Eve ate from the Tree of Knowledge, our Sages say they became like locusts whose "garments (i.e., their shells) are attached to them."[11] This can be both a positive and a negative thing. When we become innately spiritual, then our "garments," i.e., our bodies, become attached to our spiritual selves. It feels natural to us and brings us joy. If we allow ourselves to become corrupted by our impulses, the opposite is true; our physical shell clings and sticks to us to the point that we start identifying ourselves with it.

DARKNESS: SPIRITUAL LIGHT AND SPIRITUAL DARKNESS

The plague of darkness further emphasized the complete disconnect between the physical and the spiritual. Light as a representation of spiritual enlightenment, and darkness as a representation of a soulless existence, is common throughout Jewish literature. The very first time in the Torah that light is used as a reference to spiritual light is at the very beginning of the Torah when God says, "let there be light." It is there that the Sages explain that this light was not a physical light, but a spiritual light known as the hidden light, the "*ohr ha'ganuz*."

The plague of darkness wasn't just about the darkness for the Egyptians. It was about the great light that the Jewish People experienced: "People could not see one another, and for three days no one could get up from where he was; but all the Israelites enjoyed light in their dwellings."[12] This plague was a throwback to the light and darkness of the very first day of Creation when the *ohr ha'ganuz*, the hidden spiritual light, was revealed—a light that was so high and spiritual for the Jewish People operating simultaneously with a powerful darkness that was rooted deep in the spiritual realm.

Regarding the darkness of Creation, the prophet says that God "forms light and creates darkness." The words of the prophet seem strange, as darkness shouldn't need to be a separate creation; it seems to be nothing more than the absence of light. However, from a spiritual perspective,

---

11 *Bereishis Rabbah* 21:5.

12 Exodus 10:23.

the opposite is true. Godly light is always flooding everything and everywhere, and should be strong enough to wipe out any darkness. Darkness needs to be created because it filters and conceals that light to allow for our own free will.

The light and darkness in this plague represent the separation of this holy spiritual light and spiritual darkness. Most of our life is spent in confusion between what is right and wrong, true and false, holy and unholy, desirable and undesirable. But once we are ready to let go of our ego and allow ourselves to become more and more connected with our soul, we can clearly see the difference between it all. That is what was symbolized in the plague of darkness.

DEATH OF THE FIRSTBORN: REEXAMINING OUR PURPOSE

The relationship between parents and their firstborn is very deep and powerful. The firstborn represents the parents' legacy, carrying on their mission and purpose. The Egyptians put lots of focus on their firstborns, giving them an elevated status both socially and religiously. The final plague was more than just an execution of Egypt's firstborns; it was an elevation of the Jewish firstborns, and an elevation of the entire Jewish People as God's firstborn—God's purpose.

We will see in the next chapter that the death of the firstborn represented a complete cutting off of the values and the priorities of the Egyptian way of life.

By the time the night of the fifteenth of Nissan arrived, as the Jewish People sat down to their very first Passover Seder, with the blood of the Pesach sacrifice smeared on their door as a sign of protection from the Angel of Death, they were already feeling the beginning of their transformation. The four elements of Egypt had been dismantled. They were now ready for the four stages of redemption.

summary

- The purpose of the ten plagues was not only to compel Pharaoh to send out the Jewish People or to punish the Egyptians, but to drive home a powerful message about the power of transformation, specifically in the realm of the four elements.

- The first seven plagues are each connected to the four elements and contain messages of how to create transformation in each of those areas.
- After those seven plagues, there was a complete revelation that God is in control of all the elements. The final three plagues would contain their own set of messages about the nature of the soul as being a tool in the hand of God, emanating from a realm above the four elements and representing the true spiritual greatness that the Jewish People would receive as they became a holy nation.

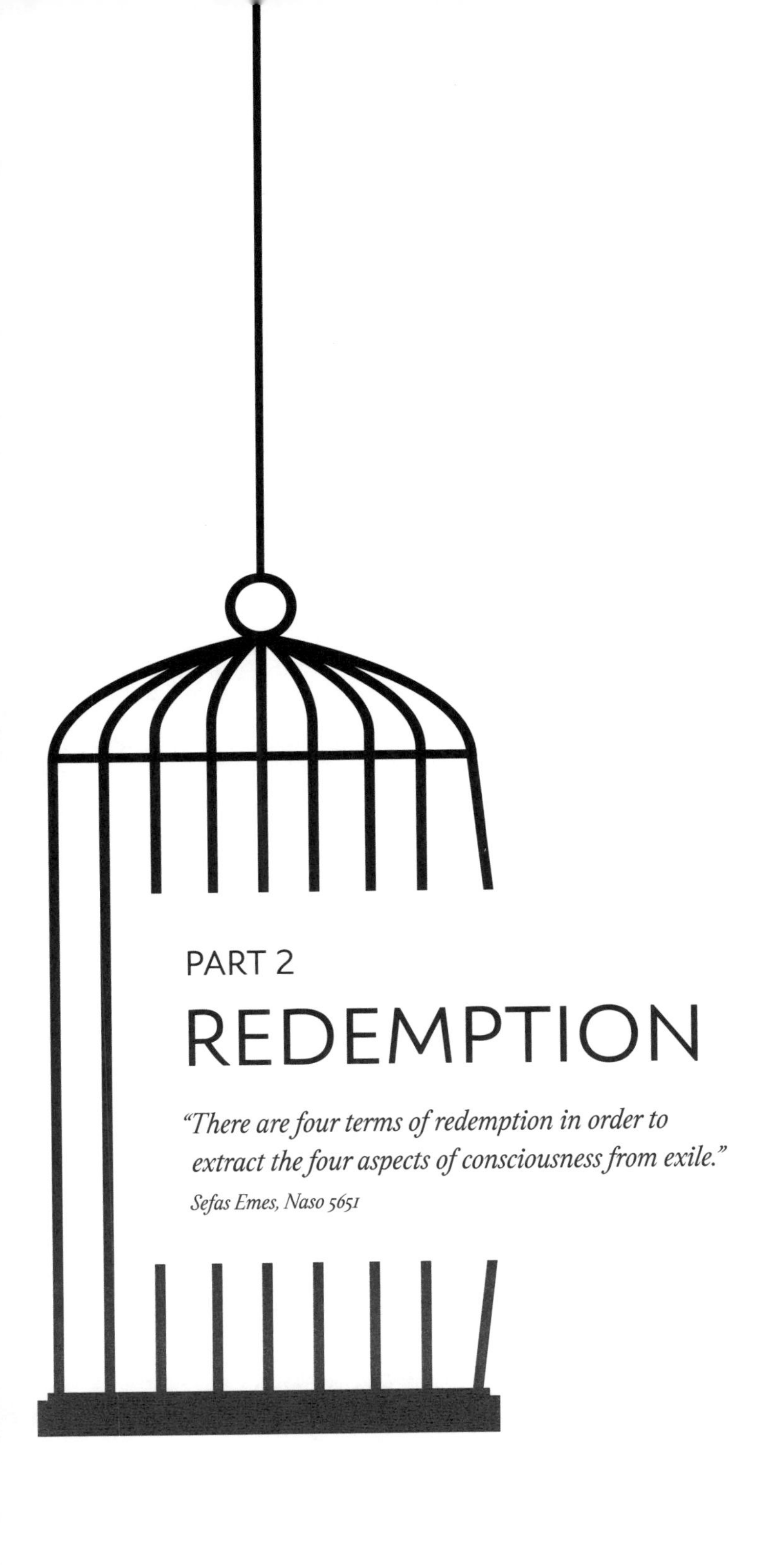

PART 2

REDEMPTION

"There are four terms of redemption in order to extract the four aspects of consciousness from exile."

Sefas Emes, Naso 5651

chapter nine

EMBRACING THE PROCESS

THE MOON'S MESSAGE

We live in an era when we expect the solutions to our problems to happen quickly. Google has conditioned us to find answers immediately. Amazon has taught us a lifestyle where anything on the planet can be delivered to our door in a matter of days or even hours. And similar services have given us the blessing of groceries and ready-made food at our door before we even realize that we are hungry.

But certain processes in our life cannot be rushed, such as healing, joy, and spirituality. They require patience, resilience, and grit.

Many people set out on the journey toward a better life to free themselves from their Mitzrayim, but only a small percentage make it to the end of the journey. Most people jump ship when things get too difficult, or when it takes too long. Those who make it to the finish line realize that it is a marathon, not a sprint. They realize that in order to succeed, you need to play the long game.

IN ORDER TO SUCCEED, YOU NEED TO PLAY THE LONG GAME.

This message was communicated to the Jewish People shortly before they left Egypt in the form of the very first commandment they were given as a nation.

Two weeks before the Jewish People left Egypt, God gave them their very first mitzvah: to sanctify the first day of the lunar cycle, the new moon, as the first day of the month.

In Jewish law, the new Jewish month is not a set day on the calendar. Rather, the High Court proclaims the start of the new month based on the testimony from at least two witnesses who saw the first glimmer of the new moon. This first day of the month is a mini-holiday called Rosh

Chodesh, and there were special ceremonies that would be performed in the Temple to celebrate the day. Prior to the destruction of the Temple, with the Jewish courts realizing that this system would not endure in exile, they sanctified the new moon in advance for future years to come and established a set calendar. Though we no longer rely on the sanctification system, we still consider Rosh Chodesh a special day, celebrating it by reciting *Hallel* (special paragraphs of Psalms) during our prayers.

It is certainly a fascinating commandment, but it seems like an odd choice as the one chosen to be the introductory mitzvah to kick off the Jewish People's mitzvah-observing experience. It must be that this commandment contains tremendous depth and that it teaches the Jewish People many fundamental lessons about Jewish life. What could this be?

For the Jewish People, the moon would become a symbol of constant renewal. It waxes and wanes, predictably reminding us that darkness is only temporary. Just when the moon seems to have faded completely into the darkness, it begins to slowly increase its light once more. The first lesson the Jewish People were meant to learn from the moon was this lesson of embracing the process. It is for this reason that we base our calendar on the moon and establish our holidays according to the lunar cycle. We are being reminded to be like the moon—to ride the waves of the highs and lows of life and to continuously renew ourselves and never fall into despair.

And even when the darkness persists, and there are times in our life when all we know is pain, the moon teaches us that it is possible to glow brightly even in that darkness. It reminds us that we have the power to persevere and even find the hidden light.

Looking closely at the words of the Torah, we find this powerful and practical message hinted to in the words of the commandment: "This month shall mark for you the beginning of the months; it shall be the first of the months of the year for you."[1] First, we see that the Torah emphasizes that this month is for **you**. This is your time. Today. So own it! Furthermore, the word for month is *chodesh*, which contains the very same words as *chadash*, newness. So, the very words of this

---

1 Exodus 12:2.

commandment contain a hidden message: this is your moment of renewal!

Two weeks later, they would be sitting at their very first Seder while still in Egypt, already celebrating their freedom while still in the place of their slavery. This was to show that for a person to fully experience freedom, he needs to truly be able to visualize it, even before it has already happened—to deeply believe it will happen to the point that we are willing to act upon it as if it had already happened.

FOR A PERSON TO FULLY EXPERIENCE FREEDOM, HE NEEDS TO TRULY BE ABLE TO VISUALIZE IT, EVEN BEFORE IT HAS ALREADY HAPPENED.

And as they are celebrating their freedom, the tenth plague is occurring. As we saw before, the firstborn represents the parents' legacy, carrying on their mission and purpose. The final plague challenges us to look at our "firstborns," i.e., our purpose, our values, and our legacy. The firstborn represents our innermost motivation, our will, our "why"!

There is much emphasis as to how this plague was specifically carried out by God himself. This hidden motivation that is concealed deep in our consciousness is completely undetectable by anyone besides the Almighty Who knows our innermost desires. To transform ourselves at this level is possible only by completely cleaving to the Divine and letting go of all attachment to ego and false beliefs.

THE STAGES OF REDEMPTION

On Passover night, our ritual is called a "Seder." The word *seder* means "order," and we are very meticulous throughout the entire evening to perform the steps of the Seder in a very specific order: we begin with the more somber steps, like dipping a vegetable into salt water to commemorate tears, and watch the Seder morph into a full-blown celebration with food, wine, and singing.

The four cups of wine are staggered throughout the Seder, each cup representing a new milestone that we have reached in that journey.

When God announced that the redemption was happening, it was with the four promises of redemption: "I will take you out…I will save you…I will redeem you…I will take you to me as a nation." As we have seen, this is the basis for the four cups of wine. We have shown how they correspond to the four elements of our inner world, which were exiled and enslaved in Egypt, and how the plagues carried with them messages specifically regarding these four elements.

According to many of our Sages, the four promises of redemption were also meant to show that the redemption itself would not happen at one time. While the Jewish People would have loved to see the gates of Egypt open up toward a seamless trek to the promised land, the reality is that the redemption would unfold in stages. In fact, it would be a four-stage process, with each term of redemption hinting at another stage in that process.

Because the slavery of the Jewish People was a slavery of the four elements, each stage of their redemption would correspond to one of the elements until they had completely discovered elevation and holiness in every one of these areas. As we explore the different stages, we will see those themes present themselves front and center, as the Torah weaves in lesson upon lesson to teach us what are the keys to reach mastery and to RULE (recognize, understand, learn, and elevate) over the four inner elements. We will see how each stage in their redemption was meant to help them overcome another one of the flaws that correspond to the four elements.

Exploring the four stages of the redemption through this lens will help us understand the depth of the redemption process and tell us about different aspects of our own personal redemption as well, which is in itself an unfolding process. We therefore need to look at each component of the four-step redemptive process as described in the story of the Exodus.

What are those four stages?

1. The first stage of redemption began at the start of the month of Nissan with the first commandment given to the Jewish People, and it culminated on the night that they left Egypt. It was on that night that they held their first Passover Seder with the Pesach offering and matzoh. This first stage corresponds to the element of earth.
2. The second stage began when the Jewish People left Egypt. They were now physically no longer under the influence of the Egyptians. But would they really be able to break ties with their

Egyptian identity, or would they be pulled right back into their previous world? This final separation would culminate with them jumping into the Sea of Reeds. This stage corresponds to the element of water.

3. The third stage would begin with the splitting of the Sea that happened by an eastern wind. At that point, with the realization that they are now really on their own, they will undergo a series of tests to challenge their resilience and resolve. This would reach its peak during the great war against Amalek. This stage corresponds to the element of wind.
4. The fourth stage happens when the Jewish People achieve their new identity with the giving of the Torah at a flaming Mount Sinai, when the Jewish People received their mission and responsibility. This stage corresponds to the element of fire.

IN THE MERIT OF THE PATRIARCHS AND MATRIARCHS

In order to fully understand the four stages, there is yet another fascinating connection we must explore. We discussed previously how the Jewish souls that were enslaved in Egypt had a deep soul connection with the early generations of mankind who corrupted their ways. We pointed out the connection between Cain and the earth element, the generation of the Flood and the water element, the people of Bavel and the wind element, and Sodom and the fire element. It was specifically in the areas those generations fell short that the Jewish souls in Egypt would have to experience and eventually extricate themselves from and elevate to their holy purpose.

This process of elevation, however, would not begin with them. In fact, the power to elevate the elements was something rooted deep in their souls from their ancestors. On a national level, the Jewish People would just be activating a gift that was part of their spiritual DNA.

If we take a look back in the book of Genesis, we find that much of the patriarchs' and matriarchs' adventures, sojourns, and struggles were each connected to one of the elements that they were meant to elevate. Those stories in the book of Genesis serve as a foundation to the stories of the book of Exodus. The book of Genesis establishes the roots of the tree that would be the Jewish nation, and the book of Exodus is the story of the branches. Just as a tree can only be as strong as its roots, and is always pulling nourishment from its roots, God places the Jewish People in Egypt precisely because their roots are strong enough to withstand all of the spiritual struggle they would endure and nonetheless come out even stronger on the other side.

Like a tree in the middle of winter, which appears dead on the surface yet all the while its sap is going deeper and deeper into the ground to solidify the roots, the Jewish People are actually getting stronger and stronger, though it doesn't appear that way on the surface. And just like a tree in the winter, which begins to revitalize through the sap rising long before we are able to recognize it, the redemption process unfolds slowly and methodically until the Jewish People are able to make a full spiritual breakthrough at Sinai, fully exposing the deep power of their roots.

As we explore the four stages of the redemption from Egypt, let's keep our eyes open to how they connect back to—and often parallel—the experiences of our forefathers and foremothers in the book of Genesis. Let's begin by seeing how the very words that God uses to describe the redemption parallels the experience of our patriarchs and matriarchs:

- The first promise of redemption, "I will take you out," can be seen as the type of redemption that Abraham and Sarah experienced. They spent the entire first half of their life living in Mesopotamia, trying to spread the message of goodness to the world. When we first hear God speak to Abraham in the Torah, it is to instruct him to leave his birthplace and go to the land of Israel.
- The second promise, "I will save you," is very much connected to the patriarch Isaac, whose whole essence is birth and rebirth when all hope seems lost. He is the miracle child born to Abraham and Sarah at an old age when they believed they were infertile. He is placed on an altar to become a sacrifice to God and is saved at the last moment.
- The third promise, "I will redeem you," is connected to the patriarch Jacob. The word "redemption" throughout the Torah is used to refer to the restoration of something or someone to its

proper place. There is no Torah personality whose life story is as connected to his sojourns and wanderings as much as Jacob: He must leave home early in his lifetime, and it is in the home of his wicked father-in-law that he builds a life for himself and develops his personality. He then returns home as a new man with a new name—Israel.

- The fourth promise, "I will take you to me as a nation," is connected to the children of Jacob, who will become the tribes of Israel. The story of the twelve sons of Jacob revolves very much around Joseph, his descent to Egypt, and his eventually becoming the viceroy of the land. The other sons would eventually join him down in Egypt, where the family of Jacob would be reunited and the seeds of the Jewish nation would be planted.

The connection between the patriarchs and matriarchs and the four elements was explored in great detail in *The Four Elements of an Empowered Life*. In the coming chapters, however, as we explore each stage of redemption and how it connects to elevating each of the elements, we will also refer back to the stories of our patriarchs and matriarchs. We will see how the adventures and struggles that the Torah focuses on when telling over their stories connect to the elevation of each of the elements.

As the Jewish People are moving from stage to stage, they are essentially following in the footsteps of the patriarchs and matriarchs, developing mastery in the very same manner. We will explore all of those fascinating connections in the upcoming chapters.

ELEMENT	STAGE OF REDEMPTION	KEYS TO SUCCESS	PERSONIFIED BY
Earth	*Ve'hotzeisi*— I will take you out	Positive mindset, enthusiasm, alacrity	Abraham
Water	*Ve'hitzalti*— I will save you	Experiencing meaningful and mindful pleasure	Isaac
Wind	*Ve'gaalti*— I will redeem you	Persevering through resistance and doubt	Jacob
Fire	*Ve'lakachti*—I will take you to be My people	Transcending the ego, elevating the material	Joseph

In doing so, we will be revealing a unifying thread that weaves together the Book of Genesis and the Book of Exodus, creating one flowing narrative that begins in the Garden of Eden and comes to a climax when the Jewish People finally achieve nationhood. And the entire story all revolves around the four elements and exists to teach us deep lessons about our own inner world.

With this understanding, we can now begin to take a much deeper look at the process of redemption, unpack the lessons that are contained within it, and apply those lessons to our lives.

summary

- The redemption wouldn't happen all at once, but would be divided into stages. This teaches us a lesson about real spiritual growth, which is slow and requires patience through the ups and downs.
- This is taught to us from the fact that the very first commandment to the Jewish People was about sanctifying the new moon. Because the moon waxes and wanes, it is symbolic of the ups and the downs that we go through in our own growth. It is also a symbol for constant renewal.
- Each of God's four promises of redemption correspond to another stage in the redemption: The first stage was to physically leave Egypt. The second was to abandon the Egyptian way of life. The third was to establish their faith in the desert and overcome any resistance. The fourth was to officially establish their nationhood and reach incredible spiritual heights at Mount Sinai.
- Each stage of redemption also connects back to one of the generations of the patriarchs and matriarchs in the book of Genesis: Abraham and Sarah, Isaac and Rebecca, Jacob and his wives, and the sons of Jacob, specifically Joseph.

chapter ten

MANIFESTING FREEDOM

ELEMENT	KEYS TO SUCCESS	PERSONIFIED BY
Earth	Positive mindset, enthusiasm, alacrity	Abraham and Sarah

THE GARDEN OF LIFE

Earth is both a symbol of life and of death. I once asked my gardener what he was going to do with a heap of *mud* that he was removing. He responded, "There is actually a lot that I can do with this amazing *soil*." I saw mud. He saw soil. I saw death. He saw life.

If you have ever tried to maintain a garden, you have certainly experienced the joy of watching the process of a seed sprouting into a small stem, then producing leaves and blossoming into a flower. And you have also seen how vegetation can die, when time, neglect, or trampling takes its toll.

When we bought our home, there was a beautiful garden in our backyard, the product of much care and attention by the previous owners. Though we had every intention of maintaining it, things got in the way, and that garden is now a heap of rock-solid earth that my sons use as a pitcher's mound. Every few months, I try to drop some grass seed there, but the soil has become so compacted that it is hard to imagine that this was ever the site of thriving life.

This is true in our lives as well. Like a garden, our lives require tending: watering, pulling out the weeds and crabgrass, and providing the conditions needed to thrive. But without the proper tending, time will take its toll.

Time does not allow for too much stagnation. It moves forward whether we like it or not and has an impact on all of existence. Everything in the physical world is constantly moving one step closer toward dying, making us wish we could only freeze time.

But time also carries with it new potential. Time is the enemy for one who is lazy, who thinks he can avoid stepping into the future. But it is the best friend to one who knows its secret: that it is actually fertile soil. There is new potential in every moment.

If we are afraid to tap into what we are being called upon to do at any given moment, if we are afraid of change, then we will fear the power of time. But if we embrace it, we will see that time is about new possibilities and new awakenings.

IF WE ARE STUCK IN THE PAST AND FEARFUL OF THE FUTURE, WE WILL SURELY MISS OUT ON ALL THE POTENTIAL OF THIS VERY MOMENT.

If we are stuck in the past and fearful of the future, we will surely miss out on all the potential of this very moment. We will miss out on all the beautiful things that are happening right now that serve as the harbinger for a better tomorrow. When we are stuck in the past, we can't expect a better tomorrow, but when we immerse ourselves in the power of this moment, we are tapping into the power of re-creation.

We mentioned above that it is the element of earth that traps us in the rat race of life, depleting our energy and making us feel that we are living in survival mode. The earth element is the part of us that allows ourselves to get stuck in our current situation, even when it does not meet our desires. We completely lose sight of the power of this moment, forgetting that the key to a bright future begins right now.

Earth on its own, without water or sunlight, shows no sign of life. One who cannot envision the potential of what the earth can produce sees nothing more than dead earth, which is nothing more than a burial place for anything placed in it. A person stuck in the earth element is always reminiscing about what was, what could have been, and what should have been, holding on to a negative outlook about the future. Cain killed Abel because he could not move beyond the pain that he was feeling at the moment. Pharaoh saw only negative in the future and therefore got stuck in his old ways, unable to see that change is possible.

To RULE over the earth element is to recognize how it affects us and to decide to wean ourselves off of this damaging mindset. Often, when we are so stressed by our day-to-day life, we miss out on being able to see that the possibility for redemption is right in front of us.

BE THE PERSON YOU HOPE TO BECOME

On their last night in Egypt, when the first stage of redemption is set to begin, the Jewish People are commanded to have the very first Seder. They would fulfill several mitzvos that night, like the eating of matzoh and the Passover Lamb sacrifice and singing praises of gratitude to God for taking them out of Egypt. These commandments teach us what it takes to set yourself free, to take the very first steps out of the stickiness of the earth element and into the space of fertile soil.

The goal of the Passover Lamb and singing praises of gratitude for leaving Egypt (while still in Egypt!) was to give the Jewish People the ability to manifest their own freedom, to visualize their redemption, and to remove the inner blockages that would stop it from happening. To manifest any sort of breakthrough, it is necessary to deeply believe that it will happen to the point that we are willing to act upon it and remove any of the negative thinking associated with it.

The laws of the Passover Lamb were specifically designed to simulate an experience of freedom. The slaughtering of this lamb was a risky process. The lamb was an Egyptian god, and slaughtering it was an insult and an affront to the Egyptian people. As the Jewish People themselves had also fallen into the lifestyle of idol worship, this was a difficult procedure for them as well. By slaughtering the lamb for the sacrifice, the Jewish People had a very concrete way for them to express that they were willing to put it all on the line and put their past behind.

TO MANIFEST ANY SORT OF BREAKTHROUGH, IT IS NECESSARY TO DEEPLY BELIEVE THAT IT WILL HAPPEN TO THE POINT THAT WE ARE WILLING TO ACT UPON IT AND REMOVE ANY OF THE NEGATIVE THINKING ASSOCIATED WITH IT.

They had to eat the lamb with the etiquette of free people, i.e., while fully dressed, their shoes and belts strapped, and their walking sticks in hand, prepared for the liberation. In order to manifest personal breakthrough, one needs to play and dress the part. To become a leader, one must carry himself the way that great leaders do. To become spiritually great, one must hold himself to the high standards that spiritual giants do. In fact, one great American entrepreneur describes how, while he was still poor, he would make sure to carry at least one large bill and wrap all the other bills in it. He wanted to get accustomed to seeing large bills as soon as he opened his wallet. He would also make sure to always tip servers on the higher end. It cost him only a few dollars more, but made him feel like a millionaire.

A community member of mine would frequently joke that if God would help him win the lottery, he would gladly make a sizable donation to a capital campaign that we were running at the time. I would facetiously respond that, perhaps, it works the other way. God is probably thinking, "You can barely give a small donation; how in the world will you have the capacity to give a larger one? First, show God that you can give generously with the resources that you have. When you open your hand to give, you are also opening it to receive even more abundance!" We still haven't seen the donation, and he still hasn't won the lottery.

WHEN YOU OPEN YOUR HAND TO GIVE, YOU ARE ALSO OPENING IT TO RECEIVE EVEN MORE ABUNDANCE!

Create a vision of the person you want to become in the future, then start acting like you are already that person today.

SEIZING THE MOMENT

There is no Jewish symbol that speaks to the struggle to elevate the earth element more than the mitzvah of matzoh. Matzoh is dough (hence, it comes from the earth) that is not allowed to sit for too long. This is because sitting around allows it to rise and become puffy and large, much like the unmotivated person who is spending too much time on the couch.

Our Sages point out that the word *matzos* (the plural of matzoh) has the same Hebrew letters as the word *mitzvos* (commandments).[1] Dough

---

1 See *Rashi*, Exodus 12:17, based on the *Mechilta*.

that has risen, on the other hand, is called *chametz*, a word our Sages use as a euphemism for procrastinating. Therefore, when the Torah teaches us not to let matzos become fermented *chametz*, it is simultaneously hinting to us to not procrastinate when it comes to doing mitzvos. "*Mitzvah ha'baah le'yadecha al* ***tachmitzenah***—When the opportunity to do a mitzvah arises, do not procrastinate."

The process of baking matzoh is fast-paced, frantic, and energetic, the opposite of the sluggish nature of the earth element. This is not to say that all of life needs to be fast-paced and frantic. In fact, often being in the moment requires us to do the opposite and slow down. But we cannot confuse being "in the moment" with being slow-paced and lazy. If the moment requires action, then inactivity is nothing more than just laziness. A lazy person is not stuck in the present. They are stuck in the past. Matzoh teaches us to strike while the iron is hot, before our inspiration cools down. *Chametz* thrives on inactivity and laziness, seeking the path of least resistance, just letting the natural process of life run its course, letting the time slip away.

Eating the matzoh would set the tone for how the Jewish People would leave Egypt. Those final moments of the Jewish People's time in Egypt would be anything but relaxing. There was no time for a long mushy goodbye. Instead, the Jewish People had to pick themselves up and rush out of Egypt. The Torah says that the Jewish People left "*b'chipazon*" (in a hurry).

The Torah is teaching us the most important secret to overcoming the inner element of earth: Get up and move as fast as you can! We all have moments of motivation that come on strong and leave as fast as they came. If we learn to capitalize on those moments and not let them fade away, we have discovered the secret to exponentially great productivity.

The great Chassidic master, Rav Tzadok Hakohen of Lublin, writes:

> *The beginning of a person's entry into service of God needs to be b'chipazon, done quickly, as we find that the very first Passover offering had to be eaten quickly, but this was not so with future Passover offerings. This is because in the beginning, a person needs to...protect the moment that the Godly desire is*

> *awakened in him and to rush after that moment...After that, however, he should continue on with patience and deliberation.*[2]

Rav Tzadok is introducing us to two different ways of approaching our growth. Each one is necessary at very specific times—at the beginning and after the beginning. There are times that we find ourselves in the middle of some sort of struggle, caught in the weeds. Then something sparks inside of us, and we have a flash of inspiration and motivation. These are the times (i.e., beginning points) when we need to act with alacrity and just jump in without asking too many questions, not to fall into the trap of over-thinking. Because we are not rooted at that moment on solid spiritual ground, too much planning will just open up room for obstacles and excuses to set in.

THE LAW OF DIMINISHING INTENT

One common obstacle is the voice that tells you that you shouldn't start on a new resolution without a fully developed plan—that it would be pointless to just jump in. This line of thinking is extremely deceiving, mainly because it is an excuse hiding in a rationale that certainly has some truth to it. Yes, plans are necessary to keep consistent; jumping in on motivation *alone* will not create sustained change; and thinking that it does is setting oneself up for disappointment. All this being said, however, there is still something powerful to seizing the moment.

WE SHIFT BETWEEN FEELING HOLY AT TIMES TO FEELING DISTANT AT TIMES. THERE IS NO CONTRADICTION, AND IT IS NOT HYPOCRITICAL.

When it comes to holy acts, the voice within may push a little harder and even accuse you of being a hypocrite. "Who are you to pretend to be something that you are not? Who are you to think that these yearnings inside of you are truly holy, when you know good and well that you are a sinner?"

There is no greater voice of falsehood than this one. The nature of a person is that we ebb and flow in our feeling of closeness to God. We

2 See beginning of *Tzidkas Hatzaddik*.

shift between feeling holy at times to feeling distant at times. There is no contradiction, and it is not hypocritical. It is how we are hard-wired. If the reason behind your actions is because they are coming from an inner desire and excitement, there is nothing purer and more authentic than that.

A close student of mine, who was raised without any religious practices, once expressed to me strong yearnings to engage in more spirituality. He was reading a lot and had begun a practice of daily meditation. He asked me what he can do to take his practice to the next level. I suggested that, perhaps, wrapping tefillin from time-to-time would be a beautiful addition to his spiritual practice. I explained to him the beautiful meaning behind tefillin: how the boxes placed on the head and arm represent connecting the seat of our thoughts and our actions with God, and how, when we wrap tefillin, we are binding our thoughts and actions to God.

But he refused to hear of it. His explanation was that "I am afraid that if I put the tefillin on once, it will be such a powerful experience for me that, if I don't continue after that, I will never be able to feel whole in my spiritual practice again."

Over the next several months, I continued to encourage him, but to no avail. Even as his daily practice started to slip and he no longer felt the same sense of meaning in his ritual, he would not allow himself to take this next step because of this fear.

This is a struggle that many of us encounter. We wait and we hem and haw until the inspiration fades and the opportunity is lost. Famed motivational speaker Jim Rohn gave a name to this phenomenon. He called it "The Law of Diminishing Intent"—"the longer you wait to take action, the less likely you are to take action." Or, as a teacher of mine would say, "never leave the site of a new idea without doing some action to move that idea forward."

Perhaps, we need to borrow a strategy from the playbook of sin and bad habits. When a person is giving in to temptation or desire, despite knowing that it is unhealthy and against his resolve, he dismisses all thoughts of the future and all possible repercussions. He doesn't bother dwelling on how he may feel afterward or how hard the recovery may be. He is completely consumed by whatever he is feeling at that moment.

But, when it comes to positive behavior, we do not always approach it with the same attitude. Were we to borrow the sinner's attitude, we may find that we have the ability to allow ourselves to become unapologetically consumed in the holy feelings of the moment—to forget our past, not think about our future, and just allow ourselves to be here, now.

A modern-day version of the Torah's idea of *b'chipazon*, springing into action quickly, was popularized by author and motivational speaker, Mel Robbins, who teaches about the power of "The Five-Second Rule." Whenever the awareness of the necessity to take action enters into a person's mind, there is a five-second window before that motivation will fade away. Therefore, a tool to prompt a person into action is to actually count down: "5-4-3-2-1," as if you are getting ready to launch a rocket into space, and then spring into action.

Whether this is waking up in the morning, starting a difficult project, stepping away from an addictive habit, etc., the act of counting down disrupts the default thinking, distracts us from excuses, and focuses our mind. The rule is based on the science that there is a five-second window between your initial instinct to act and your brain stopping you.

Human beings are creatures of habit. Our habits are stored completely in a different part of the brain from that of our conscious decision making. When we operate out of habit, our brain stops fully participating in the decision making. So, unless you deliberately do something to disrupt the habit, it will unfold automatically. By practicing the Five-Second Rule, you are disrupting those patterns and activating your prefrontal cortex, triggering the change.

Sometimes, a person can be going through a very difficult time in his life, and the earth element can be extremely heavy. I once spoke to a woman who was going through such a hard time in her life that even just getting out of bed in the morning was a major ordeal. The moment she would wake up, all the struggles and the loss in her life would immediately flood her brain. All she wanted to do was crawl back under the covers and sleep her life away. The thought of having to go through an entire day was completely overwhelming.

But she learned to use the following exercise to help her. Instead of allowing herself to become overwhelmed by all the thoughts of the day, she identified the very next thing that she had to do. She then articulated it to herself: "Just put your feet on the floor. Just walk to the bathroom." Once she put her focus on only the very next thing that she had to do, she would do the countdown—"5…4…3…2…1"—and then push herself. As the day would go on, she would build this momentum out of these small wins and eventually be able to pull herself out of this morning rut.

BACK TO THE ROOTS: ABRAHAM AND EARTH

With this understanding—that the essence of the Jewish People's first Seder night was focused on the elevation of the earth element—we can now see how this amazing moment was rooted in the energy of Abraham and Sarah, who embodied the trait of *zerizus*, alacrity. While there are many moments in their adventures where we see this, there is one incident where the Torah goes above and beyond to make us aware of this trait.[3]

In the Book of Genesis, we recall the famous story of three angels coming to visit Abraham to tell him that he will have a son—Isaac. Recall also that Abraham and Sarah have no children at this point. They are a barren couple with no real potential to be the progenitor of a nation until that day when they are informed that the process that would lead to the birth of the Jewish nation was about to begin.

This conversation would not simply happen over a cup of coffee. Instead, the Torah relates to us the scene upon the angels' arrival:

> *Looking up, he saw three men standing near him. As soon as he saw them, he* ***ran*** *from the entrance of the tent to greet them…Abraham* ***hastened*** *into the tent to Sarah, and said, "****Quick****, take three se'ah of choice flour! Knead and make cakes!" Then Abraham* ***ran*** *to the herd, took a calf…and gave it to a servant who* ***hastened*** *to prepare it.*[4]

3 A full discussion about Abraham and his connection to the element of earth can be found in *The Four Elements of an Empowered Life*.

4 Genesis 18:2–7.

The commentaries explain that the reason why Avraham wanted to serve cakes and not bread was because it was the eve of the fifteenth of Nissan, the night that would eventually become the night of the redemption, the holiday of Passover! Why would Abraham be celebrating this now, approximately four hundred years earlier? Clearly, it cannot be a coincidence that Abraham learns about the birth of his son, the progenitor of the Jewish nation, on the very same calendar night that the Jewish People would in the future become a free nation. Surely, Abraham felt it appropriate to celebrate with his own version of the Passover Seder!

With the scene set, we now have a greater appreciation for Abraham's frantic behavior on that night, hastening into the tent, rushing Sarah, and running to the cattle. Abraham was embodying the trait of alacrity, the very trait that the Jewish People would display mastery of on that night that they would be redeemed.

But there is yet something more about the history of this night and its connection to elevating the element of earth. If you recall, the earth element was contaminated by Cain, who murdered Abel in an act of jealousy over Abel's sacrifice being accepted rather than his. But one has to wonder, what sacrifice were they bringing exactly?

The answer to that question is found in the Midrash, which relates:

> *When the night of Pesach arrived, Adam said to his sons, "On this night, the Israelites are destined to offer Pesach offerings. You, too, should bring offerings before your Creator." Cain brought the leftovers of his meal—flax seed, while Abel brought the best of his flocks—lambs that had never been shorn. Cain's gift was despised by Hashem, and Abel's gift was found to be desirable.*[5]

Hence, we find the completion of a fascinating thread woven into the stories that form the foundation of humanity and the Jewish People. Cain kills Abel on the night of the fifteenth of Nissan, throwing himself

---

5 *Pirkei D'Rabi Eliezer*, chap. 21.

into darkness and depression—connected to the element of earth. The ground is cursed, symbolizing the future struggle of the earth element. On that very same night, Abraham, whose mission in life is to elevate the earth element, is told of the upcoming birth of his son and the seed of the Jewish nation. Abraham celebrates this by conducting his own Passover Seder and a very explicit display of the trait of alacrity. The fifteenth of Nissan then becomes the night that the Jewish People would become a nation by displaying that very same trait and running out of Egypt to embark on a journey toward freedom and holiness!

On the morning of the fifteenth day of the Jewish month of Nissan, the Jewish People began their journey. The Jewish men, women, and children, with their cattle laden with riches, would finally inhale the sweet smell of freedom.

Many people are just waiting around for something to happen: waiting to be discovered, to be invited, to be told. The very word *Pesach* means taking large steps forward. On the morning of the fifteenth of Nissan, Hashem got the Jewish nation unstuck. "That very day, God freed the Israelites from the land of Egypt, troop by troop."[6] Just reading the words gives you the chills. Centuries of bondage and now they are free! Seems to be a beautiful ending to a long drama, the breathtaking final scene in a tale of adventure. One can almost hear the theme song playing in the background.

MANY PEOPLE ARE JUST WAITING AROUND FOR SOMETHING TO HAPPEN: WAITING TO BE DISCOVERED, TO BE INVITED, TO BE TOLD.

But this would be just the beginning!

Sometimes, you think the villain is dead, or the game is over, or the heroes are about to live happily ever after, but then you realize that you exhaled too soon. There are still several chapters left, several minutes of play time, and lots of adventure left before the grand finale. And that is precisely where our adventure takes us.

---

6 Exodus 12:51.

summary

- The first stage of redemption, which corresponds to God's first promise of "I will take you out," occurred on the night they left Egypt. This was the elevation of the earth element.
- The goal of the commandments that the nation fulfilled that night, including the matzoh, Passover Lamb, and singing praises of gratitude for leaving Egypt, was to give the Jewish People the ability to manifest their own freedom, to visualize their redemption, and to remove the inner blockages that would stop it from happening. To manifest any sort of breakthrough, it is necessary to deeply believe that it will happen to the point that we are willing to act upon it and remove any of the negative thinking associated with it.
- The mitzvah of matzoh shows the importance of moving quickly when one is trying to begin a process of change. One has to act upon inspiration before the excuses set in.
- The events that happened on the night of the Seder reflect other events that happened on that night in the stories of Cain and in the story of Abraham.

chapter eleven

GETTING CLEAN

A SPIRITUAL DETOX

ELEMENT	KEYS TO SUCCESS	PERSONIFIED BY
Water	Experiencing meaningful and mindful pleasure	Isaac and Rebecca

CHOOSING FREEDOM

Dr. Edith Eger is a psychotherapist, an Auschwitz survivor, and author of the bestselling memoir, *The Choice*, where she documents her life story. She writes about how she went through the concentration camps as a young teen and the mindsets that helped her survive. But the true challenge of her life came not during the camps but after she was liberated. Liberation from the Nazis did not mean Edith's pain and suffering were over. "Even though I was free physically, I didn't know how to take responsibility for my freedom," she says.

This was true with many Holocaust survivors. They were handed freedom on the most external level, but they were so broken on the inside that they were never able to fully experience freedom, even years after they were liberated.

Before the Jewish People would come to Sinai, they would have to learn how to take responsibility for their freedom.

Many people who manage to free themselves from one prison find themselves jumping right into another one. I have spoken to many individuals who spent years trying to extricate themselves from a toxic situation, an abusive relationship, or an awful job, and once they managed to get out, they still had trouble letting it go. Sometimes, this even caused them to just jump right into another one. They have become attached to the pain.

Negative emotions chase us even when we are far away from the situation that originally caused them. When we can't let go of pain from the past, our disappointment about the present, or fear about the future, we are allowing something outside of ourselves to control us. The feelings of negativity chase after us and ruin our day and our moment, even when there is nothing happening right now to make us upset.

> MANY PEOPLE WHO MANAGE TO FREE THEMSELVES FROM ONE PRISON FIND THEMSELVES JUMPING RIGHT INTO ANOTHER ONE.

Over the course of her career, Dr. Eger created her own therapy style, Choice Therapy, based on the principle that freedom is fundamentally about choice: "While suffering is inevitable and universal, we can always choose how we respond." Inner freedom will not happen on its own. It is more likely that we will spend our entire life enslaved unless we are willing to take responsibility for our freedom. As Dr. Eger says, we need to choose freedom.

Dr. Eger's words echo a verse in the Torah: "And you shall choose life." Life in this context is synonymous with freedom. You might be alive, but that doesn't mean that you are "living" in the fullest sense of the word. You might be taking advantage of the very basics of what it takes to not die; you are breathing in oxygen and going through all the motions to make it from morning until you go to sleep, until the next vacation, until retirement, until death...but you are not choosing how to live. Choice means freedom. You need to have inner freedom to choose life.

That very first stage was just moving beyond the element of earth, the physical aspect of slavery. The feeling of being stuck. With no place to go. In the language of the four terms of redemption, that was God's promise that "I will take you out."

Now that the Jewish People have been taken out of Egypt, the next step is the task of "taking Egypt out of them." This corresponds to the elements of water, as it will symbolize the freedom from the temptations of Egypt and is the fulfillment of God's second promise "And I will save you." And it will occur as they stand on the banks of the Red Sea.

Shortly after they are out of Egypt, Moses gets a surprising message from God: "The Lord said to Moses: "Tell the Israelites to turn back and encamp before Pi Hachiros [the name of a location] between Migdol [also the name of a location] and the sea, before Baal Zephon; you shall encamp facing it, by the sea."[1]

Baal Zephon was an Egyptian idol, a surprising landmark for the Almighty to use to instruct the nation where to rest. It isn't long before Pharaoh gets the memo that the Jewish People have not only made an about-face in the physical direction that they were traveling, but that they have decided to make a pit stop at the foot of an Egyptian idol. The impression that the Jewish People are lost and confused emboldens him to arm himself and his army, and begin the great chase that would culminate with the famous Splitting of the Red Sea, an event that provided salvation to the Jewish People and the final destruction of Pharaoh's Egyptian empire.

We discussed earlier how, in addition to the physical slavery of Egypt, the Jewish People were also challenged to resist the temptations of Egypt, a country immersed in immorality and promiscuity. This represented the corruption of the element of water. Standing at this site called Pi Hachiros, at the foot of Baal Zephon, the last of the Egyptian idols, the Jewish People are about to be taught about what it takes to extricate oneself from the grasp of addictive tendencies.

The commentaries describe the scenery at this place called Pi Hachiros, which is translated as "the mouth of freedom," that stood at the foot of this idol. They describe it as two high rocks shaped in the form of male and female.[2]

If you have ever been to any of the national parks that feature large rock formations, you may have noticed how certain rock formations are surprisingly human-like. I remember taking a trip to Arches National Park in Utah and looking up at an incredible rock formation and thinking how it looks like three Chassidic Jews standing together engaging

---

1 Exodus 14:1–2.

2 See *Rashi* and *Mechilta*.

in conversation. I later found out that this formation is actually known as The Three Wise Men!

The Chassidic commentator, Rav Mordechai Yosef of Izhbitz, explains the deeper message behind placing the idol near this rock formation. The idol that stood there represented promiscuity and lust, hence it was very befitting to have it placed near this rock formation that appeared to be male and female, as a symbol for lustful behavior. The name Pi Hachiros, the mouth of freedom, suggests that the Egyptians' idea of freedom was the license to engage in debauchery and act in whatever indulgent way that they desired.

Why would God ask the Jewish People to make their first pit stop right here? The verses go on to say that this was meant to lure the Egyptians to chase them by making it seem like they were lost and vulnerable. But there is more. Pharaoh would have assumed that when the Jewish People see the idol of lust, it would make them question whether the lifestyle of discipline that they were entering into was really true freedom. Pharaoh believed that the reminder of the indulgent ways that they were exposed to in Egypt might make them reconsider whether this is the type of freedom they really wanted. If they would relapse, the Egyptians would be right there, chasing them to pull them right back in.

RECOVERY

The situation that the Jewish People find themselves in is symbolic in many ways to one who is trying to overcome his own entrapments, such as a harmful behavior, an addiction, or a bad habit. Just when a person feels that they have made headway and improvement, temptation comes knocking at their door, looking more appealing than ever, making it feel invincible. We are all familiar with the dangers of an addiction and how it may ruin someone's life. But what we often overlook is how the inner workings of addiction are present in all of us. We are all vulnerable to be controlled by external fixes and dependencies, and the consequences of that can be detrimental. Though it hasn't surfaced

JUST WHEN A PERSON FEELS THAT THEY HAVE MADE HEADWAY AND IMPROVEMENT, TEMPTATION COMES KNOCKING AT THEIR DOOR, LOOKING MORE APPEALING THAN EVER, MAKING IT FEEL INVINCIBLE.

in the same extreme way to completely disrupt our life, the patterns happening beneath the surface can drastically affect the quality of our lives.

The Egyptians chasing after the Jewish People, not allowing them to ever get comfortable in their freedom, is symbolic of how an unwanted behavior "chases after" its victim even once he thinks he is out, trying to pull him back into relapse, causing the feeling that it is impossible to get away.

To finally free themselves from the entrapment of the Egyptians, the Jewish People would have to take one more step forward before God would swoop in and intervene on their behalf. Facing the Red Sea and realizing that they have hit a complete dead end, they would have to give themselves over completely to God and just jump into the sea.

What were they to do at that point in time?

> *But Moses said to the people, "Have no fear! Stand by and witness the deliverance that God will perform for you today; for the Egyptians whom you see today, you will never see again. God will battle for you; you remain silent!"*[3]

This was the defining moment—the entire reason why God brought them to the sea and set them up in such a predicament. Everything until that point had been completely the hand of God. The Jewish People had not taken any active part in bringing about their own redemption. This would now be their moment. They would have to put their entire fate into the hands of God...and jump!

Here again, we can view our journey to break free from all unwanted behavior through the lens of an addict trying to overcome their addiction. We discussed in Chapter 5 how the most successful system of recovery, the Twelve Steps, was based on the powerful idea that people with a high level of addiction almost never recover without some sort of "vital spiritual experience." This is because the driving force of any sort of addiction is really to fill a void inside that is looking for a much

---

3 Exodus 13:14.

deeper connection with something bigger—a "union with God" as Dr. Carl Jung referred to it. This craving is so deep that it is causes the addict to consistently return again to something that can actually kill them just to numb this pain. The only way to quench that thirst is to deliver that spiritual fulfillment that the addict, and all of us, so badly yearn for.

One needs to look no farther than the first three steps to see the necessity for the addict to fully give himself over to a higher power:

1. We admitted we were powerless—that our lives had become unmanageable.
2. We came to believe that a Power greater than ourselves could restore us to sanity.
3. We made a decision to turn our will and our lives over to the care of God as we understood Him.

Can there be a better expression of what was happening during those moments when the Jewish People were standing on the banks of the Red Sea?

Rabbi Dr. Abraham Twerski speaks of this same phenomenon:

> *Just as the body needs certain nutrients and develops symptoms when it is deficient in an essential nutrient, so, too, the spirit needs its nutrients. If the spirit is deprived of its essential nutrients, it, too, develops symptoms, the most prominent of which is unhappiness and discontent.*

In the book *Stepping out of the Abyss*, author and addiction recovery specialist Menachem Poznanski refers to this as "spiritual deficiency disorder" and explains that

> *the only feasible approach is one that treats the core-problem—the spiritual malady—with a spiritual solution, thus neutralizing the obsession and putting the alcoholic or addict in touch with a power greater than himself.*

This yearning for spirituality is born out of the water element inside us. In Psalms, King David uses water many times as a symbol for deep yearning and prayer: "I will pour out my heart like water opposite God." Jung fascinatingly chose to close his letter to Bill Wilson, the founder of the Twelve-Step program, using yet another quote from Psalms: "As the deer yearns after the water brooks, so too, does my soul yearn after you, O God."[4]

This last verse is the perfect metaphor for the state of the Jewish People as they stand at the shore of the Sea of Reeds, sandwiched between a powerful Egyptian idol and what would soon become one of the greatest spiritual experiences mankind has ever had.

The Torah here is teaching us the true secret to real recovery from the traps of unwanted dependencies. Those who have gone through the recovery process would be the first to say that the moment they were able to admit their helplessness, and that their moving forward would only begin by giving themselves up to a higher power, that was the moment that their recovery journey began.

We are all walking around suffering from spiritual deficiency disorder. It is deeply rooted in what we are looking for in our human experience. Some people who are more deeply in-tune may feel it more and are, therefore, more prone to either fall into a state of sadness or try to throw themselves into some sort of escape. The thrill of an activity that is either dangerous or forbidden is sometimes the only experience powerful enough to temporarily drown out the feelings of emptiness that we are feeling.

THE THRILL OF AN ACTIVITY THAT IS EITHER DANGEROUS OR FORBIDDEN IS SOMETIMES THE ONLY EXPERIENCE POWERFUL ENOUGH TO TEMPORARILY DROWN OUT THE FEELINGS OF EMPTINESS.

In leaving Egypt, the Jewish People turn "their will and their life over to the care of God," and shortly thereafter, they find themselves safe and secure, surrounded by water, as their Egyptian enemies are finally being washed away.

The commentaries explain that the act of jumping into the sea was symbolic of immersing themselves in the waters of the mikvah. As we

---

4 Psalms 42:1.

saw above, the mikvah is deeply connected to love and connection, as it is the tool that reunites a husband and wife in deep intimacy and pleasure. It represents the water element channeled toward its holy purpose. While crossing the sea, the Jewish People would be purified from any residue that was left from Egypt and would discover the deepest pleasure, i.e., intimacy with God. This is for what the element of water inside of us truly yearns.[5]

BACK TO THE ROOTS: ISAAC AND WATER

It is this ability to rise above temptations to discover deeper intimate connections that is embodied by the second patriarch, Isaac. Our Sages teach that the trait of Isaac is *gevurah*, translated as inner strength or restraint. To understand this trait, we turn back to our Sages in *Ethics of Our Fathers*, who teach us: "Who is considered a person of inner strength? One who has learned to conquer his desires."[6]

To conquer one's desires does not mean making them go away; rather, it is the ability to channel them for their holy purpose—to resist when resistance is what is necessary, and to engage when that is the holy path. When an army conquers a city, the greatest expression of strength is not to destroy the enemy. It is to take the city under its control. That is true *gevurah*.

Isaac is the patriarch who, at the age of thirty-seven, was ready and willing to be brought as an offering to God, to give himself up completely. This is a symbol of complete nullification of the self, the ability to remove oneself from the physical world.

And, yet, Isaac is also the symbol of how to elevate physical pleasure. It is Isaac who asks his son to "prepare a dish for me such as I like, and bring it to me to eat so that I may give you my blessing before I die." Isaac specifically wants to give his son a final blessing over a meal, when

---

5 Our Sages further use the splitting of the sea as a metaphor for the intimacy between man and woman in the statement, "Bonding couples together is as difficult as the splitting of the sea" (*Sotah* 2a). The commentaries remark curiously about this comparison. Based on our understanding of the element of water, one can certainly see that the splitting of the sea is symbolic of the channeling of the element of water for a truly sacred purpose.

6 *Avos* 4:1.

his spirits are high and he is in an elevated state of consciousness. It is also Isaac about whom the Torah first mentions the concept of love between a man and woman in the verse: "Isaac then brought her into the tent of his mother, Sarah, and he took Rebecca as his wife, and he loved her."

Thus, Isaac teaches us the true power of elevating the water element. It is the ability to not only show restraint from the temptations of the physical world but also the ability to engage in it and use it for its highest purposes.[7] This is something that we can apply to our own life when we engage mindfully in the pleasurable activities that we are involved in.

This involves taking the time to think about what we are really trying to achieve through that activity, including the following:

- How this pleasure will give us good health or energy
- How it might strengthen us physically, emotionally, or mentally
- How it will give us the ability to appreciate the gift
- On a more lofty level, how we are utilizing and transforming the raw materials of creation into sources of strength so that we can become the best version of ourselves and serve God better

Fascinating as it may seem, according to the Midrash, that seminal occasion of the Binding of Isaac also featured its own experience of water drying up to allow him to cross. The Midrash describes how the Satan went ahead and created a river to try to prevent Abraham and Isaac from crossing. They entered until the water reached their necks. Abraham lifted his eyes heavenward and prayed, and as the Midrash relates:

> *The Holy One, blessed be He, responded: "Be assured that through you, the unity of My name will be made known through the world. Thereupon, the Holy One, blessed be He, rebuked*

7 A full discussion about Isaac and his connection to the element of water can be found in *The Four Elements of an Empowered Life*.

> *the source of the water, and caused the river to dry up. Once again, they stood on dry land.*[8]

We can now close another amazing circuit of events that happen in the Torah. The generation of the Flood caused corruption through their indulgence in the physical world, and they were wiped out. Isaac came along to begin the process of reparation by his ability to transcend the physical world and only use it for its intended elevated purpose.[9] The defining moment was the "rebirth" that happened when he was bound as a sacrifice. The Jewish nation left Egypt and was immediately tested whether they would use their freedom to engage in an indulgent lifestyle. If they would, the Egyptians would be right there to pull them right back in. Instead, they chose the path toward God, the path of elevation, the path of giving up of themselves to achieve a greater union with God.

As the waters came crashing back down on the Egyptians, the Jewish nation experienced the completion of the second stage of redemption, "And I will save you." This is symbolic of being rescued from the grasp of their impulses and temptation. But something else was happening as well. The moment that they trekked forth into the water, completely reliant on God, the next stage of redemption, "And I will redeem you," had also begun, as did the elevation of the element of wind.

summary

- The second stage of redemption, which corresponds to God's second promise, "I will save you," occurred after the Jewish People left Egypt and were standing on the banks of the Red Sea. This was the elevation of the water element.

---

8 *Tanchuma, Vayeira* 22.

9 The very name Isaac, in Hebrew *Yitzchak*, hints to his connection to the generation of the Flood. The very same letters of his name also spell "*ketz chai*," meaning the end of life, a reference to the generation that brought the end of life to the world and the necessity for its rebirth. The story of the binding of Isaac, which brought him moment away from death, was somewhat of a rebirth in its own right.

- God commands the Jewish People to camp in a location that was the site that hinted at their propensity to indulge in lustful activities. This was to allow the Jewish People to make the conscious decision that they will use their freedom to become holy and not to indulge in forbidden desires.
- Leaving the idol to jump into the Red Sea is symbolic of someone caught in their bad habits and addictions letting go of those practices and immersing themselves in spiritual experiences.
- This stage of redemption is connected to Isaac, who was the embodiment of showing restraint and of elevating desire and physical pleasure. We can emulate this as well, by learning to be mindful when we are enjoying and benefiting from physicality.

chapter twelve

RIDING THE HIGH WAVES... AND THE LOW ONES

ELEMENT	KEYS TO SUCCESS	PERSONIFIED BY
Water and Wind	Synchronizing the heart and mind (emotion with intellect)	Jacob

HEART AND MIND

Water and wind love to team up during big moments in the Torah. They are the very first elements of which the Torah speaks. All the way back before the story of Creation begins, the Torah speaks of the partnership between water and wind: "The earth was unformed and void, with darkness over the surface of the deep and a **wind/spirit** of God was sweeping over the **water**" (Genesis 1:2).

In the Creation story, the skies, which are connected to the wind element, are paired together with the waters as well. On day two of Creation, God spreads the sky to separate the upper waters and lower waters, and on day five, God creates the birds of the sky together with the fish of the sea.

In the story of Noah and the flood, the Torah teaches that, "God caused a wind to blow across the earth, and the waters subsided" (ibid., 8:1).

And it is the element of wind that plays a key role in the splitting of the sea when "Moses held out his arm over the sea, and God drove back the sea with a strong east wind all that night, and turned the sea into dry ground."

As discussed previously, the elements of water and wind correspond to the realm of emotion and intellect, respectively. When we are speaking about how they express themselves, they are very different: feelings vs. thoughts; heart vs. mind; intuition vs. logic.

But in truth, when we are speaking about refining our inner world, it is necessary to see these two elements as a team. Emotion without intellect lacks meaningful direction and is fleeting. Intellect without emotion is uninspiring and lifeless. To reach mastery in one of those realms without the other seems to be an impossibility.

The evil inclination, the bad habits, addictions, temptations, all thrive by disconnecting one's desires from his intellect. The inner Pharaoh succeeds when he can separate the heart from the head, pushing us to pursue pleasures that we know in our minds that we will come to regret. As mentioned above, the very name *Pharaoh* comes from the word *oref*, the neck, which separates the head from the heart. When we are facing temptations, the voice of reason is silenced, our higher mind is exiled and replaced by distractions, false rationales, and silliness to allow our base desires to take command of our consciousness.

EMOTION WITHOUT INTELLECT LACKS MEANINGFUL DIRECTION AND IS FLEETING. INTELLECT WITHOUT EMOTION IS UNINSPIRING AND LIFELESS.

Therefore, at this moment of redemption, the elements of water and wind synergize and harmonize, as the Israelites themselves unlock the power of holy intellect and holy emotion, developing not only a belief in God (intellect), but also a deep emotional bond (emotion) with the Almighty and with each other. "God drove back the sea with a strong east wind all that night."

As we climb the ladder toward our greatest self, we learn to fuse our emotions with our intellect to ensure that our growth will be both inspiring and enduring. Wind is the element of the intellect, and it is connected to the power of speech. The deeper we allow the inner voice of our beliefs and understandings to speak to our heart and fully penetrate into our emotions, the more we can create deep transformation.

SONG OF ECSTASY

At the sea, the Jewish People experienced the highest level of deep transformation. They saw the Egyptians drown, marking a complete cutoff from their previous life. Egypt was for them an "exile of speech" that is rooted in the element of wind. And at that moment, they opened their mouths and not only spoke but began to sing—not just any song, but a song whose every word came from a place of prophecy: "Then Moses and the Israelites sang this song to God. They said: 'I will sing to God, for He has triumphed gloriously!'"

This is the third stage of redemption, "I will redeem you with a mighty hand and an outstretched arm"! Note that, unlike the first two terms of redemption, which focused on God "taking us out **from** the labors of the Egyptians" and "saving us **from** their bondage," this redemption is neither about the past nor about any destination. It is about this powerful moment of transformation, the deep relationship that is being experienced right now. Who knows what tomorrow will bring, but right now, the Jewish People are all consumed in a state of pure ecstasy!

The gateway from a lifestyle that lacks spirituality to a more spiritually driven lifestyle often begins with a powerful experience that wakes one up and opens their mind and heart to the possibility of more.

For some, their very first trip to Israel, standing at the Western Wall for the very first time, and being brought to tears. For others, such a powerful experience may happen while they are experiencing the grandeur of nature, while others may experience it through music. Many young people have their first spiritual experience in a summer camp setting, sitting around a campfire in the open woods with friends and a few guitars, singing meaningful songs. Concerts and music festivals for some, a "*kumzitz*," "*tisch*," or "*farbrengen*" for others,[1] sitting in the synagogue with a powerful chazzan for yet others, or just sitting around the Shabbat table singing beautiful Shabbat melodies can provide this deep spiritual-emotional sensation.

In today's language, we may refer to this as a state of expanded consciousness, or even a state of ecstasy. This term "ecstasy," which comes from the Ancient Greek word *ekstasis*, means "to stand outside

---

1 These are Yiddish terms for a variety of spiritual experiences that facilitate communion and camaraderie, and feature emotional singing, sharing of Torah thoughts, and often inspirational stories.

oneself." When we experience this, our conscious mind relaxes and the subconscious takes over. This opens the door for us to experience an intense euphoria, to unlock a deeper part of ourselves of which we may have been unaware before, and to connect powerfully to a greater intelligence.

The Jewish mystics call it *deveikus*, a deep spiritual connection. At the sea, the Jewish People experienced the greatest level of pure ecstasy that humanity can experience. In our own lives, we are meant to try to find such experiences and use them to connect to our *neshamah*.

In their song, the Jewish People declare: "This is **my** God and I will glorify him, the God of my fathers and I will raise him up." Sometimes, a person who has struggled in the past may have built up some sort of resentment toward God as the concept was taught to him. Therefore, he cannot turn immediately to the God of his fathers. Instead, he needs to start from scratch, developing a new perception of what God is to him. Only later will he be able to return to what he has been taught and see what parts of that he can accept.

When we experience such moments of expanded consciousness, of clarity and deep emotion, we feel like we will never be the same again. We feel completely transformed, and it is unimaginable that we would ever look at the world the same way. But just like a powerful wind eventually passes, letting go of all of the objects that it lifted up on the way, that is true for spiritual experiences as well. Often, after the spiritual experience has passed, we can feel low again. The spiritual experience was just the beginning of the elevation of the wind element.

Now the heavy lifting begins. The spiritual high usually leaves a residue behind that can propel a person into a more motivated way of living. We can almost capture that feeling in our memory bank and pull from it whenever we feel low. But it can often feel bitter. And that is exactly how the Jewish nation felt after the adventure at the sea had passed.

THE MORNING AFTER

Rabbi and author Moses Gersht, in his book, *It's All the Same to Me*, talks about the disappointment that we often feel after an intense joyful experience:

If we crave the continuation or the intensification of a joyful experience, then when it inevitably changes, we will experience dissatisfaction in direct proportion to the strength of our craving. Thus, all negative emotions are not defined by what happens to you but by your inner response to what happens. Emotions are real, but they are not reality. They are merely the reality you still choose to see at any given moment.

This is exactly what happens to the Jewish People after emerging from the sea. They arrive at a place referred to as Marah, which comes from the root *mar*, bitter. Often the Torah refers to a location not by a name that describes the location itself, but the experience that the subject of the story will have there. The Torah says: "They came to Marah, but they could not drink the water of Marah because it was bitter; that is why it was named Marah. And the people grumbled against Moses, saying, 'What shall we drink?'"

The great Chassidic master, Rav Dov Ber of Mezeritch, points out that the Hebrew words that the Torah uses are *marim heim*, which means: "because *they* were bitter." The Torah is hinting at the truth behind why the water was undrinkable: It is because the Jewish People were bitter! The quality of the experiences in our life are directly connected to the mindset that we have going into those experiences. If we are carrying bitterness inside of us, then we will taste only bitterness in the experiences that we have.

THE QUALITY OF THE EXPERIENCES IN OUR LIFE ARE DIRECTLY CONNECTED TO THE MINDSET THAT WE HAVE GOING INTO THOSE EXPERIENCES.

Let's go back to the spiritual emotional ecstatic experience that we spoke about above. Our friend takes his first trip to Israel and is deeply moved by the Western Wall, the holy sites of Israel, and the national pride that he feels. At that moment, he feels like a changed person! How can he ever be the same! He has such clarity of what he wants his life to look like. He can visualize it in his mind's eye, and that excites him more than anything else he has ever felt in his life.

A few days later, he is back on a plane. Back in his home environment, he is doing everything he can to keep this feeling alive. He is reading books that he bought in the Holy Land, praying intensely for a few minutes every day, even designating his favorite wall and pretending that it is the Western Wall. He shows pictures and tells stories to everyone whom he meets, maintains a strict diet of falafel and shawarma, and even speaks to his Uber drivers in Hebrew!

But slowly, as reality is setting in and day-to-day life gets back to normal, suddenly the inspiration starts fading like the wind. The spiritual experience that he had was so extremely powerful and transformative, but he is having trouble re-adapting to day-to-day life. He doesn't feel so spiritual anymore. The intensity and the passion eventually go away. He knows that he can't go back to his old world, but doesn't see a path forward either. He is thirsty to feel something again. And all he tastes is bitterness.

In modern terms, we may call this stage in the redemption process "the messy middle."

The messy middle is the stage when a person begins to wonder whether he was too quick to leave his previous life and whether he has the resources to continue. He has burnt his bridges with the past but has not yet developed a vision for the future. It is scary and lonely.

And at that point, we may also feel deceived by our spiritual teachers and leaders. A congregant may look with disappointment at his rabbi and start complaining that the sermon isn't inspiring enough, or that the synagogue doesn't have enough to offer. The former yeshiva student may look back at his school years and start blaming his teachers for not giving him enough to sustain him spiritually. The one who chose a more observant lifestyle believing that every day would provide a spiritual explosion feels deceived by those who brought him closer.

Indeed, that is what the Jewish People felt after the ecstasy of the Red Sea faded. They saw the dry hot desert before them without a clear understanding of what lies ahead and from where their sustenance would come.

This is what many of us feel when we are feeling no emotion whatsoever in our Judaism. We wonder if at some point we made a wrong turn and somehow God's presence left us. We look around and feel like other people are connecting and growing, and for us everything is dry.

The Torah teaches us what our approach should be when we are feeling this spiritual void.

> *He [Moses] cried out to God, and God instructed him about a wood, and he threw it into the water, and the water became sweetened; there [at Marah, God] gave them the commandments and the laws, and He tested them.*[2]

There are several opinions about the nature of this wood. It may have been a willow, a type of bitter ivy, an olive tree, or a thistle bush.[3] But all opinions seem to agree that the wood was bitter. Why would God command Moses to use a bitter wood to sweeten bitter waters?

The Torah here is teaching a powerful lesson of how to reframe our outlook when we are facing spiritual bitterness in our lives. In a world where we are so accustomed to instant gratification, the lesson here is to learn to find the sweetness in the bitterness. That is, to recognize that the spiritual thirst itself, the discomfort of knowing that you want something more, that yearning is all part of the sweetening process.

RECOGNIZE THAT THE SPIRITUAL THIRST ITSELF, THE DISCOMFORT OF KNOWING THAT YOU WANT SOMETHING MORE, THAT YEARNING IS ALL PART OF THE SWEETENING PROCESS.

Ultimately, we will learn how to find and create those mini-experiences into our day-to-day lives and figure out what activities will help us find connection and flow. We will discover ways to inspire ourselves and remind us about these higher levels of ourselves. But until we can feel that again, we need to learn to appreciate the sweetness of bitter yearning for the feelings of closeness to God that we are currently missing. "As the deer yearns after the water brooks, so too, does my soul yearn after you, O God."

In yet another fascinating interpretation of this bitter wood, our Sages explain that the "*eitz*" in the verse refers to "*eitz chaim hi*," meaning "it [the Torah] is a tree of life." Our Sages teach that the Jewish People were

---

2 Exodus 15:25.

3 *Midrash Tanchuma*, Exodus 24.

given aspects of Torah to study there. Though the official "giving of the Torah" would happen at Sinai, this initial introduction would give them tangible ways to connect with God through their Torah study. There, they would be able to rediscover the Godly light that they experienced at the sea, and that would become a permanent part of them.

In the next chapter we will see how the patriarch Jacob represents the elevation of the wind element. The Torah describes Jacob in his early years as "a man of wholesomeness, dwelling in tents," a reference to his commitment to deep Torah study. It was because of this commitment that he was able to remain spiritually inspired, even when he was steeped in the corrupt environments that he would later find himself.

In our own journeys as well, the secret to maintaining or reawakening that closeness, even when find ourselves in spiritually void environments, is to build into our schedules time to engage in study of some sort. In Jewish tradition, the Torah is considered the most direct path to experiencing God by fusing together one's own mind with Divine intellect. Those who have made it a practice of spending time each day to study Torah—whether it is to review the Torah portion, study a piece of Talmud, read an article, attend a class, download a podcast, etc.—find that there is a constant connection, a light that doesn't burn out, that continues to illuminate their life.

WAITING TO FEEL MORE SPIRITUAL MAY ACTUALLY BE HARMFUL FOR ONE'S SPIRITUAL GROWTH.

This was God's response to the Jewish People's bitterness. Ecstatic spiritual experiences will happen in one's life, and when they do, they are beautiful. But one cannot build a spiritual regimen around waiting for it to happen. In fact, waiting to feel more spiritual may actually be harmful for one's spiritual growth if it causes frustration and even more bitterness. Instead, the Jewish People receive a gift in the form of Torah study that they can engage in every day, consistently and methodically, to slowly expand their mind and keep their hearts aflame.

summary

- The third stage of redemption, which corresponds to God's third promise, "I will redeem you," began with the wind splitting the water and continued after the Jewish People emerged from the Red Sea. This was the elevation of the wind element.

- At the sea, the Jewish People are raised to a very high level of belief that is expressed in the song of the sea. This is the first part of the elevation of wind.
- Immediately after the Jewish People emerge from the sea, they are faced with the bitterness of not being able to maintain that level. God gifts them sections of the Torah for them to continue engaging their intellect and stay connected to the spiritual experience.

chapter thirteen

RESISTANCE

ELEMENT	KEYS TO SUCCESS	PERSONIFIED BY
Wind	Persevering through resistance and doubt	Jacob

KEEPING THE FAITH

The most difficult part of an important project is the completion. For many reasons, the last 20% of big projects is often the part that has the highest rate of failure. Many new ideas, important emails, home repairs, great books, and online applications, forms, courses, and donations somehow find their way into the black hole of incompletion, never to be heard from again.

In his book *The War of Art*, author Stephen Pressfield writes, "The danger is greatest when the finish line is in sight. At this point, the Resistance knows we're about to beat it. It hits the panic button. It marshals one last assault and slams us with everything it's got." The "resistance" he refers to is what we referred to earlier as the *yetzer hara*, the negative voice inside our head.

AS WE GET CLOSER AND CLOSER TO THE FINISH LINE, ALL SORTS OF EXTERNAL AND INTERNAL OBSTACLES START GETTING IN OUR WAY.

As we get closer and closer to the finish line, all sorts of external and internal obstacles start getting in our way. The most significant of these obstacles is the feeling of doubt and insecurity. Throughout our life, this uncertainty is of the greatest hindrances to us reaching our full potential. We frequently question whether we are doing the right thing, whether we are in the right place. It is insecurity that doesn't allow us to ever be fully present with what is.

The Jewish People are at a point in the journey where they are trying to elevate the element of wind, the element that is connected to our intellect and our beliefs. In order to move forward toward officially become God's chosen nation at Sinai, the Jewish People will have to reach a level of complete faith in God with all uncertainty and doubt left behind.

At this point, the Jewish nation will be tested in this area of faith and challenged to confront any doubt that they have in the Almighty's providence. They will encounter the forces of resistance that are always strongest before the breakthrough.

Often, fear and anxiety can come from knowing something amazing is happening and we just don't feel ready, or deserving, or an active part in making it happen. The Jewish People were being swept away by a hurricane of holiness, on an adventure leading them to a place where they would have to answer to the highest standards. They were thrilled and excited, but internally they were scared. And that is when fear creeps in. This led to complaining about whatever there was to complain about, and even denying God's presence.

Their faith would be tested with three ordeals:

1. They worry about food supply. In response, God delivers the manna.
2. They worry about water. In response, God delivers water flowing from a rock.
3. They are attacked by an enemy nation called Amalek. God helps them fight and they emerge victorious.

Each of these ordeals contain powerful lessons for us in our journey as we get closer and closer to our own destination of freedom. We will look at these three stories and see what we can take away from them.

MANNA AND EMUNAH

It begins with the Jewish nation, who had left Egypt with many provisions for the way, developing anxiety about where their sustenance would come from. The Torah does not indicate that they were hungry, thirsty, or experiencing any provisional shortage—only that they began to complain.

Their frustration becomes so intense that they start making declarations that seem completely irrational. When asking for food, they go so far to proclaim: "If only we had died by the hand of the Lord in the land of Egypt, when we sat by the fleshpots, when we ate our fill of bread!"[1]

Sometimes, the fear of completion becomes so strong that we actually start looking back with nostalgia at the toxic situation that we were in, almost retroactively transforming it into a positive experience.

The Almighty would now show the Jewish nation that they are safe and secure and that His Divine hand is with them every step along the way. He would rain down a seed-like food from the sky called manna, which the Jewish nation would be able to use to form their "bread" in the desert.

The name *manna* is derived from the reaction that the people had when they first experienced this phenomenon and they cried out "*Mahn hu*," translated as "what is this?" But there is a hidden message in these words. This term *mahn hu* has the very same Hebrew letters as the word *emunah*, which is typically translated as faith.

What was this mysterious *emunah* food?

There is an opinion among the Kabbalists that manna was the food that Adam and Eve ate in the Garden of Eden when they were at the highest elevated state of consciousness! This means that it wasn't just food to feed their stomachs for which the Jewish People were hungry. It was about experiencing higher consciousness in even the most mundane aspects of their life. To eat just to feed their bodies, which would eventually die, was not enough for them. They could have done that in Egypt "sitting by the fleshpots"! In the desert, they expect more. Through the manna, the Jewish People would be groomed to reach levels of understanding along the lines of what Adam and Eve experienced in the Garden of Eden, where they saw with full clarity that everything in their life, down to the most mundane aspects, came directly from the hand of God!

While the manna fell only while the Jewish People were in the desert, the mindset that the manna cultivated is one that we are supposed to

---

1 Exodus 16:3.

carry with us in our day-to-day lives. The food that we eat, and the physical world in general, has a spiritual component that we are meant to tap into by focusing on the fact that it is all being delivered to us by the Almighty. As Rabbi Nachman of Breslov teaches, "A person needs to look at the 'intellect' that is contained in every matter" in order to really tap into the spiritual vitality it has to offer us.

THE MINDSET THAT THE MANNA CULTIVATED IS ONE THAT WE ARE SUPPOSED TO CARRY WITH US IN OUR DAY-TO-DAY LIVES.

Living life with this perspective fosters the abundance mindset that we spoke about above.[2] When we generally believe that everything we have at any given moment is truly a Divine gift, we experience a much more joyful, rich, and stress-free life. When we believe that we are worthy recipients of the Divine flow of blessings, we become a worthy vessel for that flow.

This *emunah* mindset does not mean that a person doesn't have to try hard. But it is the view that all our efforts are secondary to the real cause of good to manifest in our life. The primary cause, of course, is the hand of God. All we need to do is remove the resistance, the skepticism, and the doubt and open ourselves up to receive what the Almighty is waiting to give us. Then we can step back and allow God to fill those vessels in whatever way He sees fit.

WATER FROM A ROCK

The Jewish nation then arrives at a place called Refidim. As we saw previously, the Torah will refer to a location by the events that happen there, or even the state of mind of the people when they got there. Here, our Sages comment that Refidim is a contraction of the words *rafu yadam*, meaning they became lax in their actions, referring to spiritual pursuits. But what should they have been occupied with?

In the last chapter, we saw that the Jewish People were given selected portions of Torah study to engage in to keep their connection with God strong after they had experienced the incredible high of the splitting of

---

2 See Chapter 4.

the sea. Their lax attitude meant that they were losing interest in staying connected in this way, and therefore losing their connection to God.

This is very significant at this stage in the journey. As we have seen, the corruption of the wind element is manifested as levity, preoccupation with trivialities, and wasted time and words. Therefore, as the Jewish People are at a stage where their focus is refining the element of wind, the attitude of the Jewish People at this point makes them vulnerable to strong consequences for their actions.

The Torah says that they begin to thirst for water. Without a consistent practice to keep them connected, the passion that they felt before is gone, and they are thirsty for it. The Torah says that the Jewish People ask a shocking question: "Is God among us or not?" They are not doubting God's existence but God's presence. They want to know whether God is with them in each and every moment.

Once again, God responds:

> *Pass before the people; take with you some of the elders of Israel, and take along the rod with which you struck the Nile, and set out. I will be standing there before you on the rock at Horeb. Strike the rock and water will issue from it, and the people will drink.*

The object that must be used to deliver the water, the spiritual jolt that the people need, is the very same stick that God had commanded Moses to use to split the sea. The Jewish People need that reminder in a visual fashion to bring them back to how they felt at that auspicious moment. The water is going to come not from a lake or a spring but a rock, a symbol for stability and permanence. God's message is clear. The spiritual path is not going to be one of daily spiritual ecstasy. There are going to be stretches of time that we feel extremely uninspired, and the only thing that will keep us connected are those daily doses of freshness and new inspiration in the form of the Torah that we learn.

AMALEK

In this final challenge guiding the Jewish People to master the element of wind, they will meet a new nemesis, one whose very essence represents the resistance that we spoke about above; an enemy whose whole essence is the absolute denial of anything sacred.

"Amalek came and fought with Israel at Refidim."[3]

The nation of Amalek were descendants of Jacob's brother, Esau, and the inheritors of his hatred toward his brother's family. They attacked the Jewish People as they were approaching Mount Sinai, when the whole world was still in awe of all the miracles that had been performed on our account. The nations of that region all knew that this was our party, and that this was our time to shine! Amalek knew it, too, and they hated us for it. It enraged them. They attacked us knowing that they couldn't win, but they did it anyway because they couldn't face the truth.

In doing so, Amalek earned for itself a special place in Jewish history, forever remembered for what they did to us:

> *Remember what Amalek did to you on the way when you were leaving Egypt, that he happened upon you on the way when you were famished and weary, and cut down all the stragglers in your rear.*

The Torah's choice of words, "*Asher karcha ba'derech*—He happened upon you" or "surprised you" (*karcha* is from the root *keri*, which means randomness and coincidence), is meant to teach us the symbolism of Amalek in our life: randomness, chaos, and uncertainty.

The word "*karcha*" also has the root *kar*, cold. Thus, the verse about Amalek can be read, "Amalek cooled you off." They were like that cold wind that is the negative expression of the wind element, that resistance that hits hard when the momentum is strong.

Amalek takes on many forms in the world. But no matter what physical form it takes on, it always embodies itself as a strong force trying to stop us when we are on the verge of a major breakthrough. Amalek is anti-Semitism. Amalek is atheism. Amalek is the voice in our life that tries to hold us back from growing, that mocks us when we are trying to change.

---

3 Exodus 17:8.

Amalek is the inner voice of self-doubt.[4] Amalek is the cold force of resistance and self-sabotage that is inside of us, that icy wind that "cools us down" when we are trying to feel passion and excitement in our life.

A simplistic impression of Amalek may lead us to believe that they were not more than a gang of desert-dwelling hoodlums looking to make trouble. But they are far more sophisticated than that. The Torah refers to Amalek as the "leaders of the nations."[5] Rabbi Nachman of Breslov understands this to mean that Amalek is connected to attacks on faith and religion, such as the ones of philosophers, scientists, and atheists who use their sophisticated arguments to confuse people into denying God. Rather than seeing the powerful hand of God hidden behind the wonders of creation, they cast doubt upon everything with various alternative explanations and logic.[6]

The spiritual root of Amalek is present in other places in the Torah as well. The *Zohar* teaches us that the soul of the nation of Amalek draws its life force and vitality from the energy of the serpent of the Garden of Eden. Kabbalah says that the serpent was an angel by the name of Sama'el. The Torah describes the serpent as "clever." He confused Eve with all sorts of twisted arguments, messing with her mind, confusing her so much that she actually thought that she was doing something good. "Eat this and you will be like God." This is the power of the ministering Angel of Amalek. The snake was, therefore, cursed that he will be crushed "in the head" by the children of Eve.

Amalek is also the ancestor of Haman, the villain in the Jewish holiday of Purim. The translation of Purim means "lots" or "lotteries," a funny name for a holiday. But the concept of a lottery is that everything is left up to chance and probabilities. Nothing is Divinely ordained and therefore nothing is inherently sacred. This curse of the serpent comes to fruition in the book of Esther, the final book of the Torah, when Haman, descendant of Amalek, is hung "by his head" on the "tree" that he made for Mordechai.

---

4 The numerical value of the word Amalek equals *safek*, which means doubt (the letters of both equal 240).

5 Numbers 24:20.

6 See *Likutei Moharan, Tinyana* 19.

The manifestation of Amalek in modern times is the one who not only refuses to acknowledge that there is more to existence than the reality that he can observe with the five senses, but he mocks it and wages war on anyone who believes in the spiritual and the metaphysical. He presents his arguments under the facade that his way is more grounded and logical, while ignoring the fact that his theories require a much greater leap of faith than acknowledging the Divine intellect behind creation. As Sir Isaac Newton commented, "Gravity explains the motions of the planets, but it cannot explain who put the planets in motion."

OFTEN DOUBTS ARISE INSIDE OF US, AND WE START QUESTIONING OURSELVES AND OUR OWN BELIEFS.

In order to defeat Amalek, the Jewish People needed to strengthen their faith.[7] In our own journeys, we are also challenged to strengthen our own faith, especially when we encounter ideas and arguments against our belief in God and in Torah from people who appear to be smarter than us. Often doubts arise inside of us, and we start questioning ourselves and our own beliefs. Because we personally feel defenseless and insecure in our own beliefs, we end up retreating and starting to question ourselves, forgetting that we have a strong and rich tradition to stand upon that has withstood millennia of critique and questioning by those much wiser than us.

To question and to challenge is a virtue in Judaism, and with the proper guidance, it opens up new doors and depths. But our search should begin from a place of confidence and strength, rather than doubt and weakness. Our faith also needs to be strong enough to be able to tolerate unanswered questions and to keep at the forefront of our minds the old saying, "If we understood God, we would be God." We will always live with a certain level of mystery. And it is our choice how we will allow that to affect our life. Will we let it consume us? Or will we accept it, befriend it, and confidently move forward in our life despite those feelings?[8]

---

7 See Exodus 17:12: "And the hands of Moses were *emunah*." Literally, this could be translated as supported. Rabbi Nachman of Breslov interprets this as a symbol of *emunah*.

8 In this light, there is an old Jewish saying, "There is no joy as finding an allowance when

We do not need to respond every time that we are criticized or mocked about what we believe (either by outsiders or by the voices in our heads). Just as we are strong enough to stand up against a harsh wind without being blown over, we can stand in the face of criticism or insult and not respond. Though this might be difficult at the moment, it is a small price to pay for the feeling of strength and expansion that one feels afterward.

Defeating Amalek means that one is no longer entrapped in the opinions of others or afraid of what they will say. It means learning to live the way that resonates with you at your core, not based on the expectations of others. People will talk, judge, and criticize. A truly free person knows that it is nothing more than words—just a futile wind that will blow by and fade away.

BACK TO THE ROOTS: JACOB AND SIMPLE FAITH

It is this ability to stand strong in our faith, to refine our intellect, that is embodied by the third patriarch, Jacob. Our Sages teach that the trait of Jacob is *emes*, truth. The struggle between Amalek and the Jewish People stems from the original struggle between Jacob and his brother Esau, the grandfather of Amalek. Esau is described as a "hunter/trapper," which is understood by our Sages as having the ability to ensnare them with his tongue, to deceive others with very clever mind games and manipulations.

Jacob is identified as an "*ish tam*," a whole or a simple person. This simplicity is not rooted in the inability to think in a complex way, but rather a simplicity of pure and sincere faith. Though Jacob is described as being simple, he had the wits to outsmart all the enemies and tricksters that he had to encounter in his life.

This is the deeper understanding behind Jacob's other name, Israel, a name given to him by an unidentified "man" who challenges him to an all-night wrestling match while returning home from the house of

---

there is doubt." It is typically understand as the joy of permitting something that was in question of its permissibility. But it can also be understood as "There is no joy as the joy one feels when he learns to allow his doubt to exist." It is interesting that in the Hebrew language, the word for satisfaction and fulfillment is *sippuk*, which has the same letters as *safek*.

his deceitful father-in-law, Laban. Our Sages identify this man as the guardian angel of Esau, Sama'el, which as we saw above is connected to the snake of the Garden of Eden and the guardian angel of Amalek! Jacob emerges victorious and earns himself the name Israel, or Yisrael. The Hebrew letters of the name *Yisrael* are the same as the words "*rosh li*," my head is mine. This is a proclamation of the ability to think independently and not be manipulated by the force of Amalek and other people's pressure.[9]

The story of mankind will be one of intellectual battles. We RULE over the element of wind when we learn to stand strong with our belief, while always probing deeper and deeper. Always learning but not allowing ourselves to be blown around by the winds of doubt and heresy. Amalek is that force that will not allow us to just remain stagnant. It will either break us or propel us forward to the next level.

summary

- The elevation of the wind element continues in this chapter as the Jewish People are challenged in the desert to refine their belief in God through three events.
- The first event is regarding the deliverance of food, which comes down in the form of the manna. This Eden-like food of faith was meant to instill in the Jewish People that God's presence is eminent in even the most mundane aspects of life.
- The second event features water flowing from the rock to quench the thirst of the Jewish People. Our Sages understand this as being a spiritual thirst after feeling distant from God.
- The third event features the Jewish nation waging war against their archenemy, Amalek, who represent the cooling off of inspiration and the insertion of doubt into one's faith. The war is an outgrowth of an earlier struggle between Jacob, the man of truth, and his brother, Esau.

---

9 A complete exploration of the connection between Jacob and the element of wind can be found in *The Four Elements of an Empowered Life*.

chapter fourteen

BEYOND YOUR EGO

ELEMENT	KEYS TO SUCCESS	PERSONIFIED BY
Fire	Detachment, moving beyond the ego	Joseph

CHILDREN OF PROPHETS

We all have a little prophecy inside of us. The great Chassidic master, Rabbi Klonimus Kalman Shapira, known as the Piaseczna Rebbe, would often quote our Sages who say, "If we are not prophets ourselves, we are certainly the children of prophets." He would encourage his students to view themselves as such and try to discover the spark of prophecy that is inside of them. When he would see doubt in their eyes, he would remind them that prophecy is not about receiving Divine messages about what will happen in the future or being able to perform great miracles. It is about rising above one's ego to access a higher spiritual consciousness.

WE OPERATE FOR THE MOST PART ON A VERY LOW PLANE OF CONSCIOUSNESS, AND OFTEN FORGET THAT WE WERE MADE FOR MORE.

All of us have the innate ability to reach great heights in our consciousness. If we properly channel the energy of our minds, we can transform it into a vessel for deep spiritual awareness. We can access great innate wisdom and clarity, seeing the world through a much more broadened perspective. We can generate deep compassion, love, and connectivity to others and to ourselves. We can awaken the joy, positivity, and expansiveness that lives inside of our hearts.

Yet, we tend to channel most of our mental energy toward the more mundane aspects of life: paying our bills, running our errands, and getting through our daily to-do list. Hence, we operate for the most part on a very low plane of consciousness, and often forget that we were made for more. We are driving 30 mph in a Bugatti, not even realizing that we are behind the wheel of a machine that can hit 300 mph. We are standing on the top of the Swiss Alps, but are too distracted by our phones to notice the scenery.

This is the next step in our journey from Egypt to Freedom, the ability to RULE over the element of fire, and the fulfillment of God's fourth promise of redemption, "and I will take you to me as a nation." The element of fire is about self-actualization and discovering an authentic greatness. In our own personal journey, this fourth stage is when we achieve clarity of purpose and authentic self-worth.

When we lack purpose and self-worth, we take aim at the things that society tells us are the definitions of success and feeds our ego, as we spoke about previously. As the author Eckhart Tolle writes:

> *Whatever the ego seeks and gets attached to are substitutes for the being that it cannot feel. You can value and care for things, but whenever you get attached to them, you will know it's the ego. And you are never really attached to a thing but to a thought that has I, me, or mine in it.*

Nothing can satisfy us, though, until we turn our attention inward to the fire that is inside of us, and walk on the path of authentic self-actualization and true purpose, letting go of attachment to the things that are nothing more than external facades.

The elevation of the element of fire is taught to us in context of the next step in the journey of the Jewish People when they became a holy nation at the foot of Mount Sinai.

> *Moses brought the people out toward God from the camp, and they stood at the bottom of the mountain. And the entire Mount Sinai smoked* ***because the Lord had descended upon it in fire****, and its smoke ascended like the smoke of the kiln,*

> *and the entire mountain quaked violently. The sound of the shofar grew increasingly stronger; Moses would speak, and God would answer him with a voice.*[1]

The Mount Sinai experience is connected to the element of fire because it is there that the Jewish People accepted on themselves the mission of becoming "a kingdom of priests and a holy nation." Their role was to set the world ablaze with spiritual fervor. It is there that their souls were lit on fire, and they discovered the deepest levels of holiness. At Sinai, every Jew experienced the highest level of prophecy, hearing the voice of God calling to them. They returned to the consciousness level of the Garden of Eden with complete revelation of their connection to God. They experienced the true purpose of their existence.

The Torah itself that was given at Mount Sinai is also compared by our Sages to the element of fire: "The Torah given to Moses was written with black fire on white fire."

The *Zohar* explains this phenomenon of black fire and white fire. The black fire (i.e., the red or blue fire that we are accustomed to) is "an instrument for destruction and death, devouring whatever comes near it. But the white light above neither consumes nor demolishes, nor does it ever change."[2] The Torah, as well, has an aspect of "black fire" in the practical, hands-on details, the laws and rules, traditions, and meaningful practices. The "white fire" represents the more hidden and mystical aspects of the Torah that relate to our spiritual awareness and to our higher consciousness.

Mount Sinai was chosen for this moment not because of its grandeur but because it was the lowest of the surrounding mountains, thus displaying that a spiritual fire can only burn on something void of ego. To let go of the ego is to allow oneself to let go of the false notion that we must always be in control and that we know all there is to know, and to realize that we are just one moving part in a very sophisticated piece of machinery that is being operated by the Almighty. This is what is

---

1 Exodus 19:17–19.

2 *Zohar* 1:51a:9.

called by the Jewish mystics, *bittul ha'yesh*, nullification of the self or dissolution of the ego.

In this chapter, we will see how this experience is one that we, too, can establish at various moments in our life, recreating small Sinai moments as we go through our day.

LET GO AND LET GOD

When the Almighty offered the Jewish People the Torah, they responded with two powerful Hebrew words that echo throughout all of history: "*Naaseh v'nishma*—We will do, and we will listen." To "do" is to show a complete devotion to performing the commandments. To "listen" is to delve into the depths of the messages that are being communicated to us by God. By showing their readiness to commit to "doing" even before they understand why they are doing it, the nation showed a complete trust and devotion to the plan, even if it would at times be beyond their understanding.

Bittul, self-nullification, does not mean that one doesn't realize his own self-worth. On the contrary, it is a recognition that we have a holy fire that resides inside us when we are willing to "let go and let God" run the show. There are times in our life when we feel that things are slipping out of our control; we are stressed, anxious, and afraid. But if we close our eyes, breathe deeply, and remind ourselves that no matter what, we are being carried by a force that is so much bigger than the challenges in our life, we can experience the true bliss of self-nullification.

EGO IS NOT ONLY ABOUT ARROGANCE. IT IS ALSO ABOUT SELF-ABSORPTION OR OBSESSION WITH ONESELF.

Ego is not only about arrogance. It is also about self-absorption or obsession with oneself. A person can think very lowly of himself and still be struggling with ego because he is so self-absorbed in his own world. He is not able to think about other people because his whole world revolves around himself and his issues.

I often think about an anecdotal story about a fellow who receives an invitation in the mail to a wedding of the child of a close friend. Instead of rejoicing, he is immediately filled with all sorts of questions: "Why was I just sent an invitation like everyone else? As a close friend, certainly I should have been notified personally. Maybe we are not as close as I thought. And why is there no mention of any sort of honor at the wedding? Maybe he doesn't really want me there at all!" He decides that while he will make an appearance at the wedding, he will come significantly late and only stay for a short time.

Another close friend also receives the invitation and, having no expectations to receive any honor or accolades, is simply filled with joy and informs the host that he will be coming and how excited he is.

The time of the wedding comes, and as the host looks around, he sees only one of his friends present and immediately offers him an honor at the ceremony, to which he graciously agrees. By the time the other disgruntled friend shows up, his presence is barely noticed. His initial sour feelings are now compounded by the fact that not only is no one giving any notice to his arrival, but the other friend has been called up for an honor! He cannot even bear to be in the room for the rest of the ceremony.

For the rest of the evening, the two friends will have completely different experiences. The friend who came with joy is right there in the mix showering the bride, the groom, and the host with best wishes and blessings. He then escorts the host to the ballroom and is offered a seat at a prominent table right next to the host! By the time the dancing starts, he is already part of the family, and is being pulled into the center of the circle by many of the family members who now know him.

WHEN WE LIVE WITHOUT A TRUE SENSE OF PURPOSE, WE GET CAUGHT UP IN HARPING ON THINGS THAT REALLY DON'T MATTER MUCH AND EXIST SOLELY IN OUR HEADS.

But the disgruntled friend will remain on the sidelines for the rest of the evening. By the time he reappears, there will be no room left at the prominent table, so he must take a seat with the other acquaintances and "regular" guests. By the time the music begins to play, he feels more distant than ever before.

The difference between these two profoundly different experiences had to do with nothing more than a difference in their immediate reaction and the level of self-absorption. The disgruntled friend got caught in a web of bad decision-making, all because of the initial response of his ego.

When we live without a true sense of purpose, we get caught up in harping on things that really don't matter much and exist solely in our heads. We are much more sensitive to people not showing us the honor that we believe we deserve or giving us the attention and accolades that we would like. When we live with purpose, we have a much greater ability to completely disregard the typical metrics that many of our peers would consider success and be fully confident in who we are and what we represent.

ONE MAN, ONE HEART, ONE SOUL

Our Sages teach that angels were sent by Hashem to give two "crowns" to every individual who stood at Sinai, each corresponding to one of the two statements "we will do and we will listen."[3] "Crowns" are understood in mystical Jewish thought as symbolic of higher and expanded consciousness. The double crown that they received at Sinai refers to an extremely exalted state. It was specifically in this moment when the Jewish People let go of everything external that they were able to find their fire, their point of self-actualization, and discover the royalty inside of them.

In addition to the inner greatness that one feels when they learn the art of *bittul*, ego-nullification, there is also a deep sense of connectivity and unity with the others in our life and in our community.

The great Chassidic master, Rav Tzadok Hakohen, points out that a crown is a symbol of royalty, indicating that the crown bearer has an elevated status. There is very little value of a crown if everyone has one. It's like giving the losing team a trophy so that they won't feel bad. It would seem that the symbolism of a crown is meaningless if every single Jew has the same one.

Rav Tzadok explains that at Sinai, as the Jewish People reached a level of ego dissolution, it was revealed that every single individual has a specific mission and, in some way, is in fact the "king of the world" in that

---

3 *Shabbos 88a.*

specific area.[4] At that moment, they were able to understand not only how they personally were uniquely great, but they were able to see it in the people around them as well. The greatest sense of unity came about not because they all viewed themselves as the same as everyone else, but because they were able to identify how every single individual is absolutely unique.

When the Jewish People arrived at Mount Sinai, the Torah refers to the entire nation as one single individual: "and *he* encamped opposite the mountain," prompting our Sages to comment that at Sinai, they were like "one man with one heart"—complete connectivity. Those who master the art of ego dissolution will unlock the power of empathy and compassion and see themselves as one with the world around them. The very word for encamped, *va'yichan*, shares the root of another word in the Torah, *chein*, which is the inner grace and sweetness of an individual. At Sinai, every Jew saw the sweet essence of those around him and their unique purpose.

"Like one man with one heart" isn't simply flowery language for unity. It is a very precise language. Kabbalah teaches that every single soul comes from that original soul of man, each one corresponding to another aspect of the soul of Adam and Eve like different pieces of a puzzle. When they let go of their ego and realized how each one of them is unique in a much more spiritual way, they came together like the "one man," that one unified soul that existed in Garden of Eden—no higher or lower, just pure connection.

OUT OF BODY

Our Sages teach that the souls of those who stood at Sinai left their bodies. This is the highest level of mystical experience one could have, reminiscent of Adam and Eve in the Garden of Eden. The Torah teaches that in the Garden of Eden, Adam and Eve were unclothed, and it was only the result of the sin that their nakedness became an issue. This

---

4 To quote the great fifteenth-century Kabbalist, Rabbi Isaac Luria, known as the *Arizal*: "No two people are similar from the day that man was created and onward, and one person cannot fix what is the responsibility for another to fix."

nakedness represents a complete detachment from anything physical. They had no need for clothes because their bodies were nothing more than a vessel to transport them. Only after they sinned and began to identify themselves as bodies did they need clothes, which further became their sense of identity.

The anecdotal story is told about a group of strangers who were traveling together to tour a foreign city. At one of the stops, as the group disbanded to do some individual site-seeing and shopping, one of the women on the trip decided to change her clothing, including removing a hat and sunglasses that she had been wearing prior to that. When the group reconvened, she was unrecognizable to several of the other participants, who reported to the tour guide that one of the participants was missing. They did their best to describe her based on the clothes that she was previously wearing and other features the way they remembered them.

The tour guide frantically announced to the entire group, asking if they can all help the search to find a woman who met the description. The woman herself, not recognizing based on the description given that the missing person was actually her, joined in the search.

After several hours of an unsuccessful search, as the frustrated woman was about to give up, it suddenly hit her like a ton of bricks! The missing woman that she was looking for was actually herself! Imagine the shock. Imagine the joy. Imagine the embarrassment.

This story carries a great lesson for those who define their identity based on externals that others have provided. When that is our sense of self, we get frustrated when we feel like we are failing to find what we are looking for. But there are moments in our life that we get a lightning bolt of clarity, a deep sense that there is more to us than that. Imagine the shock! Imagine the joy! Imagine the embarrassment—to realize that that whole time we were looking for ourselves, and we were never lost.

The Hebrew word for clothing is *beged*, which comes from the same root as rebellion, because externals are a symbol of the lowering of consciousness and the false association with the physical world. It also points to the fact that clothing can be from the most deceptive aspects of a person's identity because it calls focus to the most external layer of the person, often causing a distraction from seeing their deeper essence.

It was this body identification that the Jewish People transcended when they stood at Sinai. The Torah says that the shofar blew at Mount Sinai. The shofar teaches us the role of the body vis-à-vis the soul. The shofar is nothing more than a hollow shell, yet it transforms a fleeting breath into a powerful victory cry. This communicates to each one of us that when we make ourselves hollow, letting go of our egos and relinquishing the false sense of control, only then can we fully experience the spiritual essence that is inside of us.

WHEN WE MAKE OURSELVES HOLLOW, LETTING GO OF OUR EGOS AND RELINQUISHING THE FALSE SENSE OF CONTROL, ONLY THEN CAN WE FULLY EXPERIENCE THE SPIRITUAL ESSENCE THAT IS INSIDE OF US.

Commenting on the verse, "Lift up your voice like a shofar,"[5] one of the early Chassidic masters, Reb Avraham Chaim of Zlotchov, writes: "When we view ourselves like a shofar that has no voice besides for what is blown into it—in that we have no power outside of what God gives us—we can awaken the Divine love and bring upon ourselves great kindness and compassion."

AN EXERCISE IN NULLIFYING THE EGO

All of the Torah's powerful imagery that we have been discussing—the fiery mountain, the black and white flame of the Torah, the crowns, the out-of-body experience, the shofar, etc.—can all be used to try to recreate the Sinai experience in our daily lives.

By taking some time out of our day to quiet our mind and try to get a deep-felt sense of that inner fire, we can relieve so much of the anxiety, stress, pettiness, and frustration that is borne out of the ego and awaken a calmer and elevated version of ourselves. When we close our eyes, it signals to our mind that we are ready to go deeper inward. When we take slow breaths inward and outward, we are like the shofar, hollowing out our egos to make space for the Divine love and flow. And

5 Isaiah 58:1.

when we accept upon ourselves that our greatness comes from the fact that we are part of a much bigger master plan that comes from the Almighty, and we are ready "to do" what we need to do, "and listen" in the deepest way, we are placing the crown of higher consciousness upon our heads, allowing us to fully experience our true royalty.

We spoke earlier in this chapter of the Torah being a combination of "black fire," a fire that is an "instrument of death and destruction," written on "white fire," which "neither consumes or demolishes" and doesn't change. On a spiritual level, one would say that the black fire, which is changing, is symbolic of our lower soul, which must be refined and elevated or it will become an instrument for destruction and death. But above that is the white fire, the amazing human spirit that we can discover when we let go of our ego and allow ourselves to merge together with God.

ONLY A TRUE SENSE OF PURPOSE CAN MAKE SENSE AND INTEGRATE ALL OF THE VARIOUS DIFFERENT SHADES OF OUR LIVES.

Elevation of the fire element is about learning how to tap into this higher white fire—when we can step out of the colorful details of our life and focus on the big picture. White light contains all the colors of the spectrum. It represents the inclusivity of all the other colors. Only a true sense of purpose can make sense and integrate all of the various different shades of our lives. Have we identified what we want that big picture to look like? Or are we too caught up in checking off the boxes? When we look in the mirror, do we only see what is tangible and external? Or do we see the white fire of potential?

There is a part of every single one of us that is ready to transcend all the limitations of our bodies, feelings, and thoughts. There is a part of us that exists in that place of true bliss and connection. That part of us is all will. It speaks only the language of love and yearning—not a love that is conditional or selective. It is a sea of love that includes anyone and everyone. It is in this space that we stop seeing the physical matter of the world but, rather, the Divine energy that pulses through everything and unites everything. It is the point when all fear melts away and we are filled completely with awe for the universe. It is the true elevation of the element of fire that the Jewish People achieved at Sinai, and it is what we must strive for and yearn for in our daily lives.

As with the previous stage of redemption, this newfound level of holy achievement would not go uncontested by the forces of resistance, i.e., the *yetzer hara*. To truly master the element of fire, it would be necessary to not only detach oneself from materialism but also learn to elevate it and transform it into holiness. Unfortunately, the Jewish People faltered in this area at first with the sin of the golden calf, but then they found a new opportunity in the building of the Tabernacle.

We will discuss both events in upcoming chapters. Before that, however, the story of the Exodus and our exploration of the four elements would certainly be incomplete were we to not explore the themes of the Ten Commandments that were spoken at Sinai and the depth of their message. These ten statements were what the Almighty chose to communicate to the Jewish nation at that incredible moment when they were in the highest state of consciousness. Surely, it must carry with it messages that will be central to the perfection of our inner world, and the elevation of the four elements. The central theme of the Ten Commandments will be the subject of the next chapter.

summary

- The fourth stage of redemption, which corresponds to God's fourth promise, "I will take you to me as a nation," occurs as they accept the Torah (of fire) at the fiery Mount Sinai.
- The highest level of prophecy and complete out-of-body experience that they have at Mount Sinai is meant to teach us to strive to achieve the highest levels of consciousness by letting go of attachment to physical matters and moving beyond our egos.
- We cannot define ourselves by the material objects that we have, or the status symbols that we are given. We need to view ourselves as spiritual beings with the physical world as nothing more than an outer garment.

chapter fifteen

THE HIDDEN THREAD OF THE TEN COMMANDMENTS

THE TABLETS

You've probably heard the joke about how Moses was way ahead of his time. After all, he was the first person to download data to his Tablet from the cloud. (He also taught us the importance of a forty-day warranty.) That joke will never get old. But, joking aside, the tablets that contained the Ten Commandments are definitely the most timeless principles that the world will ever know. The Ten Commandments form God's vision for a perfect world, and therefore, a mission statement for the Jewish People.

As we saw earlier, the number ten is significant as it is a reflection of both the ten utterances through which the world was created as well as the ten plagues through which the redemption process commenced. All three of these occasions contained a creative process: With ten utterances the world was created. With ten plagues, humanity became aware that there is an omnipresent force in the world that is in complete control of every element of creation. With the Ten Commandments, a vision for a utopian world was established.

THE TEN COMMANDMENTS CAPTURE THE ENTIRE JOURNEY THAT WE HAVE BEEN ON THUS FAR.

Like all of Torah, these statements contain layer upon layer of depth and meaning. In many ways, the Ten Commandments capture the entire journey that we have been on thus far. Our journey began in Egypt in a state of constriction, and it then reached its climax as we reached the height of self-actualization and transcendence of our ego. The Ten Commandments begin with the reminder that God took us out of Egypt and culminate with the prohibition to covet the status symbols that we see in the lives of other people.

The chart below shows the Ten Commandments in the format that they were presented on the tablets. As Hebrew text is written from right to left, the column on the right represents the first five commandments, and the column on the left represents the next five:

LEFT TABLET	RIGHT TABLET
6. Do not murder.	1. I am God who took you out of Egypt.
7. Do not commit adultery.	2. You shall have no other gods besides Me.
8. Do not steal.	3. Do not use My Name in vain.
9. You shall not bear false witness against your neighbor.	4. Remember the Shabbat day and keep it holy.
10. You shall not covet.	5. Honor your parents.

On the surface, the Ten Commandments seem to be ten different statements without a strong thread that connects one to the next. The commentaries see, however, several patterns that create a flow and relationship between them.

If we look closely at the deeper message and the underlying thread of the Ten Commandments, we can see that this doctrine is establishing key mindsets to really live a life of mastery. In this chapter, we will explore the structure of the Ten Commandments and the principles that are at its core.

The first clear pattern one may observe is the breakdown between the first five written on the right tablet and the second five written on the left tablet. The first five relate to our relationship with God (the inclusion of honoring one's parents in this group will be explained shortly) and the second five deal with how to treat fellow human beings.

Many of the commentaries also see a deeper connection in how they are written, in that each commandment on the right tablet is actually related to the commandment that is parallel to it on the left tablet. This in itself is a wonderful lesson! In order for us to really understand how to relate to God (right tablet), we can apply principles from relationships that we are much more familiar with, relationships with other humans (left tablet). And in order for us to really value and see human beings through the proper lens (left tablet), we need to see them as a piece of God (right tablet).

Another angle to understand the progression is to use our model of the four elements. Looking closely, we see that on each side of the tablets, the commandments are addressing the struggles within the different realms of our inner world, advancing from earth, to water, to wind, to fire!

TABLET #1: RELATIONSHIP WITH THE ALMIGHTY

Let's first see the progression on the first side of the tablets:

I am God who took you out of Egypt.	Earth
You shall have no other gods besides Me.	Water
Do not use My Name in vain.	Water/Wind
Remember the Shabbat day and keep it holy.	Wind
Honor your parents.	Fire

COMMANDMENT #1: BELIEVE IN GOD AND YOU ARE NEVER STUCK

The Almighty opens up the Ten Commandments with a bold introduction: "I am God who took you out of Egypt, from the house of slavery." The commentaries debate whether there is a commandment here at all. They also take note of the focus here: Who took you out from being slaves, rather than Creator and Sustainer of the world, which one may argue is a more foundational and impressive accomplishment. The reason behind this choice of words is because we are trying to establish more than just faith in a Creator, but instead a dynamic relationship with the Almighty that we are trying to experience at every moment. It is because of this dynamic relationship that we are able to turn to God when we are in our own personal Egypt, our own place of entrapments or limitations.

The earth element was the element of sadness and sluggishness. It was the element that kept us trapped in our physical limitations, a constant awareness of our mortality. The first commandment is a reminder that we are never stuck. The first commandment is to believe that God is there to help you rise above your challenges and break free from the things in life that you feel are limiting you. It is obligating us to believe that there is an all-powerful hand in our life that can extract us from any place at any moment to help us break free and reach our potential.

COMMANDMENT #2: DON'T CHEAT ON GOD

The second commandment, "You shall have no other gods besides Me," takes our understanding of God beyond just a general relationship but to that of a very intimate and exclusive one. God goes so far as to phrase things in a way that is surprisingly human-sounding, "For I, the Lord your God, am a jealous [impassioned] God." Certainly, God is a transcendent being, with no human emotions, and certainly, none so petty as to become jealous. And yet, to fully drive home the point of how much God wants an exclusive relationship with every single one of us, God "borrows" a human attribute with which we are familiar, as it usually applies to a spouse who believes that the significant other may be looking outside the marriage for satisfaction. Perhaps, we can even say that jealousy channeled properly in the context of marriage is the one time when it is not only appropriate but beneficial. That feeling of not wanting to see spouses lay their eyes on another should propel the parties in a marriage to try to rekindle their passion in order to avoid any future infidelity.

To further strengthen this theme, this commandment is juxtaposed opposite the prohibition of "Do not commit adultery" on the left tablet. Hardly a surprise here. The thread between these two parallel commandments gives us a heightened perspective both on how to view our relationship with God—as an exclusive "marriage-like" relationship—and on the Godliness within the relationship of marriage, as we will see shortly.

The water element, as we have seen, is the element of passion and pleasure. It is both the symbol of deep love within a marriage, as well as the stolen waters of forbidden pleasure. It is a symbol for yearning and for prayer. It, therefore, very much relates to this second commandment.

COMMANDMENT #3: SANCTIFYING GOD WITH YOUR WORDS

The third commandment to not "use God's name in vain" is also a reflection of our active relationship with God. We know that so much of what builds and destroys our intimate relationships is our words. This includes both how we speak to a person as well as how we speak about that person. The utterance of God's name is a powerful tool to channel God's presence into the world. Abusing it is a complete disregard of something that is sacred and doing so shows that we really do not take the relationship seriously.

EVERY ACTION IS EITHER GOING TO BRING HONOR OR DISGRACE TO GOD'S NAME.

Because of this, we can see the third commandment as being connected to water, because it is a reflection of how we feel about God. We can also see its connection to wind, the element of our intellect and our speech, because it is connected to the power of our words.

What is powerful as well is that the literal translation of the words is "Do not carry the name of God in vain." On a deeper level, we are being commanded to realize that we "carry" the name of God with us, in that we are God's representatives in this world. Therefore, every action is either going to bring honor or disgrace to God's name. Our job is to teach the world that the Torah's ways are sweet, its paths are peaceful, and our relationship with Hashem is one of love and connection. The third commandment teaches us to realize that we are part of something big.

COMMANDMENT #4: KEEPING SHABBAT IN YOUR THOUGHTS, WORDS, AND DEEDS

The commandments continue with the commandment to "Remember the Shabbat." The laws of Shabbat, which minimize one's interaction with the mundane and pull us out of the day-to-day grind, are an expression and a declaration of how we see God's hand in everything. We firmly believe that we can disengage from the mundane world, push the reset button, and allow ourselves to be carried by God.

This alone forms the connection between this commandment and the wind element, which is connected to our intellect and beliefs. But that connection is strengthened with the Torah's phrase "Remember the Shabbat." Memory is a faculty of the intellect. Remembering the Shabbat is about changing our thought patterns to fully experience the serenity of Shabbat. According to our Sages, Shabbat is meant to be in our thoughts the entire week, such that when one finds something special, whether it be a special food or new piece of clothing, one should set it aside to be enjoyed on Shabbat. And when it comes time for Shabbat, remembering Shabbat is about settling our minds from all of the distractions of the week and just being calm, focused, and present. The calming and focusing of our thoughts are connected to the element of wind.

Furthermore, this commandment goes beyond simply thinking about it, as our Sages gave us a very formal way to fulfill this commandment, i.e., by reciting *Kiddush*. By doing so, we verbalize (as wind is connected to speech) and bear testimony that God is the true source of sustenance in this word—not us.

COMMANDMENT #5: HUMBLING YOURSELF BEFORE YOUR ELDERS

The next commandment is to "Honor your father and mother." In addition to the practical aspects of gratitude to the ones who brought us into the world, there is an additional aspect that is being developed. The commentaries point out that this commandment would seem to be more suited to be on the left side together with the commandments that are interpersonal, rather than on the right side that are about connecting between man and God.

It seems, though, that hidden in the requirement to show respect to those who gave us life on a physical level is the ability to look upwards, to our roots, to our deeper identity, which will ultimately bring us to honor God. Being in the presence of one's parents should be the ultimate experience of humility because they are a reminder of a time when we were helpless and completely dependent on others. Therefore, we find that even great people, successful people, and powerful people feel more humbled when their parents are present.

We have seen that the element of fire is about letting go of the ego. If we can hold on to this feeling of humility and remember that we are constantly in the presence of our spiritual parent, God, who breathes life into us at every moment, we would carry with us that humility all the time!

Additionally, we saw that the element of fire connects us to the highest levels of our consciousness, allowing us to fully actualize our potential. In Kabbalah, the higher levels of one's consciousness are also referred to with the terms "father" and "mother." Therefore, this commandment may have in it the hidden message that if we can let go of our ego and become humble, we can also access these exalted states!

TABLET #2: INTERPERSONAL

This brings us to the second tablet and the series of commandments that are about interpersonal relationships. Here, too, we will see the progression of the four elements:

Do not murder.	Earth	
Do not commit adultery.	Water	
Do not steal.	Water	
You shall not bear false witness against your neighbor.	Wind	
You shall not covet.	Fire	

COMMANDMENT #6: DO NOT DESTROY THE GODLY SPARK IN EVERY HUMAN

The sixth commandment is "Do not murder." Murdering another human being is obviously one of the worst crimes that one can commit. It is cruel to the person whose life is being cut short, robbing him of the opportunity to live out his life, and causes unfathomable pain to loved ones left behind. In the story of Cain and Abel, the very first brotherly interaction recorded in the Torah ended in murder. As we saw earlier in this book, Cain's behavior is rooted in the element of earth, as it stemmed from his lack of belief in himself and his inability to move past his feelings of negativity for his brother. The first act of murder was rooted in the earth element, and it is that element that produces the jealousy, hatred, and lack of value for life that can cause any act of murder.

But the connection to the earth element goes deeper. One may wonder why this commandment should be on the list of the core ten when it is so blatantly obvious due to its cruel and barbaric nature. But, in truth, this commandment extends beyond the obvious scenarios to many more cases that need to be analyzed and scrutinized with the utmost sensitivity.

What about if we remove the cruelty and barbaric nature? What about if the human being would like to die? What about if there is no potential left in this person because he has stopped functioning? What if there are no loved ones? What if the person is in pain, and the loved ones just want to see the end of the suffering? What argument can be made to keep this person alive?

A HUMAN LIFE IS VALUED NOT FOR WHAT IT PRODUCES BUT SIMPLY FOR ITS PRESENCE HERE, WHICH IS GODLY.

In order to give us a new perspective about life, the sixth commandment is written directly parallel to the first commandment on the right side. Every moment that a human life is present on this world, it is acting as a channel for the Divine to be present on this world. A human life is valued not for what it produces but simply for its presence here, which is Godly. The heaviness and darkness that comes to us from the earth element comes from the most physical and dense part of our makeup, and therefore, only sees life for what it can contribute to this earthly world. We can only make life and death decisions by focusing on the Godly aspect of a human that transcends that.

COMMANDMENT #7: MAINTAINING THE HOLINESS OF MARRIAGE

The seventh commandment, "Do not commit adultery," is, as mentioned above, written parallel to the second commandment of not serving other gods. By connecting these two, we see that our intimate relationships are infused with God's presence. As our Sages teach us, when there is peace in the home, it is as if God's presence dwells among a husband and wife. And when there is lack of faithfulness, there is no greater desecration of God's name.[1]

Infidelity is referred to by our Sages as "stolen waters," as it is the corruption of the water element and the realm of emotion, passion, and pleasure.

This is emphasized in the Torah's account of the *sotah*, the woman who is suspected of infidelity, who after being warned to stay away from another man is observed by witnesses to have secluded herself with that man. When the Temple stood, she would be brought there and given bitter water to drink, which had dissolved within it ink that had written God's ineffable name and which would reveal the truth of her actions. If the woman was guilty, the water would cause her—and the man with whom she committed the act—to suffer a very painful death. But if she was innocent, the water would cause her to receive great blessing for her and her marriage. As we saw before, the usage of God's name is not to be taken lightly. Moreover, there is an explicit commandment against erasing God's name. Yet, this ritual reveals to us that when marriage is on the line, so is God's name, and better to erase it to restore order in that home. We see, once again, the parallel between the God-man relationship and the marriage relationship, and how it is connected to the element of water.

COMMANDMENT #8: SETTING BOUNDARIES

The eighth commandment, "Do not steal," is a reflection of one's inability to control his desires and set healthy boundaries. As in previous commandments, if the commandment was about armed bank robbery, that would be obvious. The theft we speak of here refers to kidnapping of another person, robbing them of their rights, as well as any usage of another person's property in a way that was unintended by the owner. Even borrowing someone's possession without permission is problematic. It shows a lack of boundaries.

Both the seventh and eighth commandments are connected to the element of water and follow the pattern that we have seen until now. If

---

1 *Sotah* 17a.

we rewind back to the early generations of the Torah, we are remanded that both sexual immorality as well as theft were present in the generation that was destroyed by the great flood. The flood waters were the measure-for-measure punishment for the generation that violated these two commandments (which clearly should have been part of expected ethical behavior, long before the Torah was given).

COMMANDMENT #9: UPHOLD THE TRUTH

The ninth commandment, "You shall not bear false witness against your neighbor," focuses on our responsibility to maintain and uphold what is truth. The courts are a place where truth certainly matters most, and words of testimony are in many ways some of the most substantial words that a person can speak, as the stakes are high. Therefore, it is connected to the element of wind, our search for truth, and the power of our speech.

A functional court system is meant to establish a society of people who live together as a community by setting laws, enforcing obligations, and in modern times, defending rights. False testimony creates a society of falsehood and corruption, as with the Tower of Bavel, a society that had banded together around false ideas and that was punished by being broken apart and disunited.

Though this commandment itself is about bearing testimony in court, in principle, the commandment is once again showing us the importance of searching for truth both in our beliefs and in our words. It is written parallel to the commandment about remembering the Shabbat, because just as Shabbat is our way of testifying to our belief that God is in charge of running the world, and it is our words that usher in that holiness, this commandment, as well, is meant to focus our attention on the holiness and power of our words.

COMMANDMENT #10: DON'T DEFINE YOUR SELF-WORTH WITH MATERIALISM

The final commandment, "You shall not covet your neighbor's house: you shall not covet your neighbor's wife, or his male or female slave, or his ox or his ass, or anything that is your neighbor's," speaks once again to the ability of letting go of one's ego, which is connected to the element of fire. As we mentioned above, when one does not have a healthy self-esteem, he will define his self-worth by material objects. It isn't necessarily an attachment to the object itself as much as it is the desire to be seen by others as powerful or successful. This was the corruption of the city of Sodom, to the point that our Sages teach us that the Sodomites were represented by the adage, "What is mine is mine, and what is yours is yours." Therefore, the commandment specifically focuses on not desiring what you see someone else has. It is a charge to view one's success not in comparison to anyone else, but by looking at one's own predicament.

The parallel between honoring one's parents and not coveting someone else's wealth also drives home the message that just like we didn't choose our parents, as they are handpicked by God to be our family, so too, our current predicament, home, family, wealth, etc., are all tools given to us for the sake of maximizing our potential and succeeding in the life mission that is unique to us. We need to look no farther than the tools that we are given to be successful.

OUR CURRENT PREDICAMENT, HOME, FAMILY, WEALTH, ETC., ARE ALL TOOLS GIVEN TO US FOR THE SAKE OF MAXIMIZING OUR POTENTIAL.

As we look back at these Ten Commandments, we can now view them through a new lens and understand the deeper message of what God was trying to communicate to the Jewish People and why specifically these commandments were presented to the Jewish People at this moment in time. In many ways, they had just completed the journey out of Egypt. They had accepted the Torah and stepped into their Divinely ordained mission. The Ten Commandments were a way to show them that this mission is about refining the four elements—both in their relationship with God and in their relationship with others.

summary

- The doctrine of the Ten Commandments is God's vision for a perfect world. The tablets are divided between the first five, which are about our relationship with God, and the second five, which are about our relationship with other human beings. The tablets also have a parallel structure that allows us to see similarities between each commandment and the one written parallel to it.

- If we look at the deeper message of each of the commandments, we can also see that each of the tablets develops a progression of development of the four inner elements and paints a picture of the perfected inner world.

chapter sixteen

THE GOLDEN CALF OF MODERN TIMES

ELEMENT	KEYS TO SUCCESS	PERSONIFIED BY
Fire	Elevating one's material	Joseph

FALLING OFF THE MOUNTAIN

Every destination is just the beginning of a new journey. As long as we are walking, talking, and breathing, there is always a sense that there is more to see and more to do. We are always climbing higher and higher on the mountain with our vision toward the top, but as soon as we get close to what seems to be the climax, a new peak becomes apparent, and new challenges present themselves. Sometimes, we lose our footing and free-fall to what feels to be an embarrassingly far distance from the top.

IN OUR SPIRITUAL JOURNEYS, WE MAY GET A TASTE OF A VERY HIGH SPIRITUAL LEVEL, ONLY TO FIND NEW CHALLENGES WHEN WE GET THERE.

In our spiritual journeys, we may get a taste of a very high spiritual level, only to find new challenges when we get there. As spiritual seekers, we have the innate ability to taste spiritual levels that are beyond our capacity to maintain, for the purpose of giving us an experience of the destination for which we are meant to strive. Rather than it being some unknown mystery place that seems beyond our grasp, it now becomes familiar territory. We are thirstier for it, knowing how sweet it is. And we feel more confident that we can access it, since we have been there before. In many ways, it becomes part of us so that we aren't trying to access something new—just re-awakening something that we once had.

Though the Jewish People received this very high level at Sinai, it would be short-lived. The test of the golden calf would occur only forty days after receiving the Ten Commandments, and the results would be catastrophic. The Israelites, now officially the Jewish nation, were still camping at the foot of Mount Sinai, eagerly awaiting Moses's return to the camp from atop the mountain, where he had been since the Sinai experience. According to their count of the days, Moses, who was expected to be back by day forty, was late, and they feared that he had died atop the mountain. Assuming that Moses was irreplaceable by another human, they felt that they needed some sort of physical representation of the Divine energy that was present throughout the Exodus, so they fashioned a calf out of gold and turned it into a deity.

The story of the golden calf is one that leaves us scratching our heads. How could the Jewish People commit what seems to be such an obvious and grave sin so shortly after reaching such a high level? Our Sages and the commentaries discuss this at length, offering many different interpretations, each one cluing us in on another aspect of the incredible depth of this story. In this chapter, we will strive to offer a relevant and deep angle to this story that fits our approach of seeing these stories through the lens of the four elements.

THE GOLDEN CALF DEMYSTIFIED

As we saw previously, when the Jewish People stood at Sinai, they mastered the element of fire. We saw how, in Egypt, the element of fire, which is connected to will and self-actualization, was corrupted by ego and infatuation with their wealth and abundance. A very central purpose of the Israelite exile in Egypt was to "purify the wealth" by learning a healthy relationship to all the gold and silver that was amassed there. According to Jewish wisdom, this is in fact the highest level of spiritual achievement. Rather than having to live a life removed from the possibilities of abundance in this world, the true spiritual achiever becomes a channel of abundance coming from a holy source. As our Sages teach us, "The Holy One, blessed be He, rests His Divine Presence only upon one who is mighty, wealthy, wise, and humble."[1]

When the Jewish People stood at the fiery Sinai, they achieved mastery in the realm of fire by completely transcending their ego. And while this certainly represents the first step to mastering the fire element, the ultimate goal is to be able to take that experience and integrate into the world of dollars and cents, of business deals and designer brands. For it is one thing to feel detached from the physical world when you are in the middle of having a spiritual experience in the middle of the desert. But for the one who is blessed with financial success and material abundance and still never loses sight of what the real prize of life is, that is even another level of greatness. This will be the message that is woven into the story of the golden calf.

ONE WHO IS BLESSED WITH FINANCIAL SUCCESS AND MATERIAL ABUNDANCE AND STILL NEVER LOSES SIGHT OF WHAT THE REAL PRIZE OF LIFE IS, THAT IS EVEN ANOTHER LEVEL OF GREATNESS.

One can immediately sense the symbolism in the Jewish People falling prey to worshiping a god made of gold and how that relates to this stage of the Jewish People's journey. In fact, many years later, when Moses would be giving his final speech to the Jewish nation before their entry into Israel, he would refer to this location as "Di Zahav," the place of sufficient gold, a veiled reference to the fact that it was the abundance of gold that they brought out of Egypt with them that blinded them from the truth and triggered the sin of the golden calf.

So, with the symbolism of gold certainly making sense to us as being the obvious choice to challenge the Jewish nation at this stage in their development, we may now turn our attention to the other factor here: why a calf? What is the symbolism there?

There is, in fact, deep symbolism to the calf. The ox is a symbol used throughout the Torah to represent material abundance. In fact, it is even a symbol for Egypt, which was the wealthiest country in the

1 *Nedarim* 38a.

world, as in the verse, "Egypt is a handsome heifer,"[2] or in the famous Chanukah poem *Maoz Tzur*, where Egypt is referred to as "*malchus eglah*," the empire of the calf.

One can attribute this to the fact that cows and oxen were the most valuable piece of machinery for farming, as well as a source of meat and milk. But there is a more Kabbalistic understanding as well to the connection between oxen and abundance.

Jewish liturgy speaks of a spiritual phenomenon called the "Divine throne" or the *Kisei Hakavod*. Just as a throne is a chair upon which a king sits when interacting with his subjects, the Divine throne in the spiritual realm is where the presence of God sends Divine energy into the world, like an interface level between God and the physical world. The throne symbolically has four images on each of the four sides, representing the different attributes that emanate from this holy source. One of those four images is an ox, and it is from there that blessings of physical abundance enter into the world.[3] Hence, the ox is a symbol for blessings of abundance.

With this in mind, we can now take a much deeper look at the story of the golden calf and how it fits into the entire Exodus narrative. The Jewish People were at a place in their journey where they had gone from rags to riches, from slaves to millionaires, but they must bring their expanded Sinai consciousness back into reality to show that they have fully perfected the fire element and can live as a perfected nation.

Until that point, all their sustenance had been delivered to them by Moses, his staff, and a host of miracles. What would happen, though, if all that were to disappear? Would there be Divine blessing on their handiwork, on their business deals, on their inventions, and on their technology without Moses present? The nation made the golden calf in the hope that it would be a channel for blessing. But in doing so, their actions symbolized a very common trap that many fall into when they experience such abundance in their life. They begin to forget about the

---

2 Jeremiah 46:20.

3 See Ezekiel, chap. 1, for a full description of the *Kisei Hakavod* and the ethereal beings that surround it.

Source and begin to worship the golden calf, in other words, the product rather than the source.

It is certainly no secret that we live in a society that idolizes financial success and turns billionaires into celebrities. Society pays lip service to "money can't buy happiness," but then it neglects the parts of life that do bring happiness for the sake of making more money. So often we observe those climbing the ladder of financial success only to see the entire world of their personal life crumble: marriages suffer, children not able to relate to the world in a healthy way, distrust amongst friends, etc.

SO OFTEN WE OBSERVE THOSE CLIMBING THE LADDER OF FINANCIAL SUCCESS ONLY TO SEE THE ENTIRE WORLD OF THEIR PERSONAL LIFE CRUMBLE.

The story is told about a billionaire who was on vacation on a beautiful island. He observed a local fisherman lying on his boat and enjoying the fresh air. The billionaire approached the fisherman and asked him why he isn't trying to catch more fish. The fisherman replied he had already caught enough fish for the day.

The billionaire felt the need to motivate this young fellow to work harder and replied, "It's still early enough in the day, and you can still catch a lot more fish."

The fisherman looked confused, "What will I do with more fish?"

The billionaire replied with a hint of snarkiness in his voice, "You can sell them and make more money."

"What will I do with all that money?"

"You can hire workers to do the work for you."

"And what will that accomplish?"

"That's obvious. The more people that you have working for you, the more that you are free to sit back and relax!"

The fisherman looked the billionaire straight in the eyes and responded: "Isn't that what I am doing right now?"

This witty tale tells a sad truth about the dangers of serving a golden calf and losing focus. It is the story of those who throw away the best years of their life with the hope that they will retire rich, only to spend their retired years wishing they had their younger years back. It is the story of those who are in the office so that they can take a nice vacation, and spend their time on their vacation thinking about matters that relate to the office. It is the story of those who think that they can buy the things that money can't buy.

BACK TO THE ROOTS: JOSEPH AND THE HEAVENLY CHANNEL

Our understanding of the connection between Egypt, the golden calf, and the element of fire presents us with yet another important connection. At each stage of our journey, we saw echoes of the character traits of the patriarchs who embodied mastery of that element: The alacrity of Abraham elevating the earth element, the inner strength of Isaac elevating the water element, and the simple faith and integrity of Jacob elevating the wind element.

Earlier, we mentioned how the attributes of Joseph were connected to the element of fire, as he was the fearless, humble leader who, despite his wealth and power, remained humble and God-fearing. He mastered the art of completely moving beyond his ego. Joseph is the Torah's symbol of one who uses wealth to support others, as he did in Egypt, and uses positions of power to wholeheartedly lead others.

When the Jewish People stood at Mount Sinai and received the Ten Commandments, our sages associate that moment with Joseph, proclaiming that "this one fulfilled everything that is written here" and then goes on to enumerate each of the commandments and the role that they played in Joseph's life![4]

Fascinatingly, Joseph himself is significantly connected to the image of the ox. In Genesis, his father Jacob in his end-of-life blessings hints to this connection,[5] as does Moses in his end-of-life blessings to the

---

4 See *Sotah* 13b and *Rashi* there.

5 Genesis 49:22.

Jewish People.[6] When he is sold down to Egypt as a slave, he is elevated to great power after he interprets Pharaoh's dream *about oxen* and their symbolism to the future sustenance of Egypt and their entry into years of plenty and years of famine. And Joseph becomes the conduit for Heavenly material blessing to flow into Egypt from a holy source rather than the impure source to which Pharaoh was connected!

And, when it came to the creation of the golden calf, the Midrash relates that the golden calf came into being in a supernatural way. The Midrash teaches about a rebellious Jew who "had in his possession a 'divine name' and a plate upon which Moses had written: 'Come up, ox, come up, ox!'" in order to raise the coffin of Joseph, who is compared to an ox, out of the Nile. He cast the plate into the melting pot, and the calf came out.[7]

Without the proper foundation, the Midrash is extremely enigmatic. What is the connection between Joseph and this golden calf? But it all makes perfect sense to us now, fitting together like a glove. The ox is the Heavenly sign for sustenance. Joseph is represented by the ox because he had the ability to access that Heavenly flow and elevate it. Those present at the creation of the golden calf tried to forcibly access that same Heavenly flow, but because it was not done in a proper way, it led to a corrupt, almost pagan-like, outcome.

The events at the golden calf showed that the Jewish People still needed more refinement to truly be able to fulfill their mission of elevating the entire world and the materialism that it contains. Moses would plead on their behalf for God's forgiveness and then break the first set of tablets, officially severing that initial connection that the Jewish People had with God. The spiritual crowns were removed from their heads. They lost their Eden-like consciousness.

But, as is always the case after a fall, God would give them an opportunity to pull themselves out of the mud and start to rebuild. And in this case, it was quite literally a building campaign. The atonement would come in the form of building a temple for God, the Tabernacle, or

6 Deuteronomy 33:17.
7 Also cited by *Rashi*, Exodus 32:4.

Mishkan, which would serve as a response and a rectification for the sin of the golden calf. The atonement for the golden calf would come about by the Jewish People showing that just as wealth and material blessing can cause corruption, it can also be used for its holy purpose.

FIERY MONEY

The golden calf led to catastrophic consequences, the most significant of which was a loss for the Jewish People of the crowns, i.e., the transcendent consciousness that they accessed at Sinai. The element of fire had once again become corrupt, and the nation would need to take another step to perfect it again to the best of its ability. They would need yet another way to display that all heavenly abundance was indeed given to us for the sake of elevation.

JUST AS WEALTH AND MATERIAL BLESSING CAN CAUSE CORRUPTION, IT CAN ALSO BE USED FOR ITS HOLY PURPOSE.

The Tabernacle was made of all sorts of expensive material, including "gold, silver, and copper; turquoise, purple, and scarlet wool; linen and goat hair; red-dyed ram skins, *tachash* skins, acacia wood; oil for illumination, spices for the anointing oil and the aromatic incense; *shoham* stones and stones for the settings..."[8]

Every facet, measurement, and detail of the Tabernacle would have deep symbolism of our material world and how it can be infused with holiness. The Tabernacle was the ultimate expression of the elevation of the material world.

In order to build the Tabernacle, a capital campaign would be necessary, as well as the institution of an annual tax collection. This collection would become an annual event during the Jewish People's time in the desert and in Israel while the Temple stood. The collection would require every single Jew—rich and poor alike—to donate a half-*shekel*. The half-*shekel* collection would be used to build the sockets that were the foundation of the Tabernacle, and in future collections would be used for the Temple service and the upkeep of the *Mishkan*/Mikdash.

---

8 Exodus 25:3–7.

The Sages teach us that God actually showed Moses how this half-*shekel* coin would look in a heavenly vision, where it appeared as a coin of fire that was removed from under the heavenly Throne of Glory.[9] The symbolism of the words of our Sages once again fits like a glove with our understanding of where the Jewish nation is up to in their mission.

Moses had blamed the golden calf on the riches that the Jewish People had amassed. In his worldview, he began to see money as evil, the source of all pain. God showed him the fiery coin that came from under the throne to show that money, which is deeply connected to the element of fire, can indeed be the cause of much pain, but it can also be used to create, protect, and nourish. It can come from the holiness that resides beneath the Throne of Glory.

Often people define themselves by their money. If one's money is a testimony to what he is contributing positively to the world and serving other human beings, it is certainly something in which to take great pleasure. The heavenly image of the coin of fire was taken from under the Throne of Glory, the same location from which the soul of each human being is rooted, according to Kabbalah. We are each given our unique gifts and talents through which we can offer something to the world of value and get paid for it. Our job is to use it properly: to create with fire and not to destroy with it. Our fire is meant to be the fire of the burning bush that illuminates but does not destroy. The Tabernacle would be the great symbolism of this message; it would be more than a building, but a model for what the fully whole and enlightened human must look like. The Tabernacle was not only a building for God to reside in, but a pipeline for God to reside in the human beings who connected themselves to it.

WE ARE EACH GIVEN OUR UNIQUE GIFTS AND TALENTS THROUGH WHICH WE CAN OFFER SOMETHING TO THE WORLD OF VALUE AND GET PAID FOR IT.

9 *Midrash Tanchuma, Ki Sisa* 9.

summary

- In our spiritual journeys, we may get a taste of a very high spiritual level, only to find new challenges when we get there. This is what happens after the Jewish People reach the highest spiritual level at Mount Sinai. Only a short while later, they fall back down spiritually with the sin of the golden calf.
- The sin of the golden calf is connected to the element of fire. Gold is a symbol for wealth, and the calf in Kabbalah is also symbolic of abundance. Worshiping the golden calf is symbolic of the idolization of money and power that is so prevalent in society.
- The calf is also a symbol for Joseph, who embodied what it means to use money and power to become a humble and caring leader and taking care of others.

chapter seventeen

SANCTUARY IN MY HEART

THE PURPOSE OF BUILDING A TABERNACLE

Anyone who has ever built or renovated a home is familiar with the overwhelming amount of detail and decision-making that goes into it. There are the obvious things, such as measurements of each room and the location of the various appliances, but there are also the small details that, perhaps, one has never even given much attention to, such as the style of the drawer knobs, banisters, and the moldings on the ceiling. There are hundreds of possible paint colors to choose from, and there is even a deep psychology behind each color. Who knew that some colors make us feel happy or sad, calm or excited, and even hungry or satiated?!

But a home is a home, and it speaks volumes about those who dwell in it. There was even a recent personality system, Snoopology, developed that can tell you about your personality based on "snooping" around your personal belongings and seeing how your home is set up! We, therefore, want to get it right.

When it comes to building God's house, the Torah is certainly very clear about the importance of every detail. There are more Torah portions and verses that describe the details of the Tabernacle than most of the foundational stories in the Torah.

One has to wonder what the purpose of studying so many details about the Tabernacle is when even those who read home design magazines for fun can become exhausted from it. Clearly, there must be deep symbolism to what the Tabernacle represented! In this chapter, we are going to explore the Tabernacle and see how it has profound significance to understanding our own inner world and personal growth.

Throughout our discussion, we have been learning about the transformation of the various inner realms to become vessels for holiness: the earth-body element through taking action in the moment, the water realm by channeling our passion into powerful ecstatic experiences, the intellect through deep faith, and the fire element through moving beyond our ego and trying to tap into a greatness that is bigger than anything spiritual.

When we transform each inner realm, we can fully experience the fifth element of our inner world—our Godly souls that we spoke about above. We are now ready to receive the gift of the *Shechinah*, the Divine Presence dwelling in our hearts. This is the ultimate purpose of Creation, and it was expressed by the Tabernacle. As we explore the Tabernacle, we will see how all of the lessons of the four elements were present there, and how the Tabernacle as a whole represents the inner wholeness that we have been speaking about throughout this book.

WHEN WE TRANSFORM EACH INNER REALM, WE CAN FULLY EXPERIENCE THE FIFTH ELEMENT OF OUR INNER WORLD—OUR GODLY SOULS.

Our Sages teach that God created the world for the purpose of having a place to dwell in the lower physical realms. The primary place of that dwelling is in the heart of mankind. On Day Six of the Creation story, God found that abode when he blew of His essence into Adam and he became the first soulful human being. But it wouldn't last. Adam and Eve sinned, and their level of holiness was drastically decreased. The vessel for God's dwelling was shattered.

Some 2,448 years later, the Jewish People stood at Mount Sinai and heard the word of God. Once again, God had found his earthly abode. But it wouldn't last either. The Jewish nation sinned with the golden calf, and their level of holiness drastically decreased. The vessel of God's dwelling was shattered, as were the two tablets that they were meant to receive.

A few months later, on a day that would be considered for the rest of time a day of atonement, i.e., Yom Kippur, Moses brought down a second set of tablets to replace the first broken ones. A few days later, the Jewish People began a massive building project. The goal of this building project is articulated in the verse, "Make for me a holy space and I will dwell among *them*." Using the term *them* rather than *it*, God emphasized that the ultimate destination is still meant to be the heart of mankind, not simply a constructed building. Even in Jewish life today, the holiness of a synagogue, place of worship, or house of study, is not the primary residence of the Almighty. The address for that is inside you and me.

One of the great spiritual teachers would tell his students that as a child, he would ask his father, "where can God be found?" His father would respond that God is everywhere. But something about that answer did not resonate with the young boy. One day he returned to his father and said, "I have figured out where God is...God is wherever you let him in!"

The purpose of the Tabernacle, then, was to be that place where God would always be "let in" because of the holy vessels and services that would be done there. But, on an even deeper level, the holiness of the Tabernacle was powered by the actions, feelings, thoughts, and yearnings of the Jewish People. It would be a central point where Heaven and Earth would meet, where prayers would ascend from below to Above, and where prophecy would descend from Above to below. And, like an electrical power grid sending electrical currents across the grid, the Tabernacle would send out waves of spiritual energy throughout the nation.

It would not necessarily be large, but it would be beautiful. Every single detail would be Divinely ordained and contain multiple symbolisms—from the shape to the size, to the materials used. It would be a portable home, with a courtyard, a sanctuary, and an innermost chamber called the Holy of Holies. Each section would have its unique furniture, and different aspects of worship would happen in each of these spaces.

THE FOUR ELEMENTS IN THE TABERNACLE

Since the Tabernacle represented God's dwelling in man, it was only fitting that every detail of it should represent the form of man in some way. And because the human being is a composite of the four elements, it would only be befitting that the Tabernacle would be full of symbolisms of the four elements and how to reach a state of mastery in those areas.

Upon approaching the *Mishkan*, one would already encounter a symbolism of the four elements. The roof of the Tabernacle was made of fabric curtains that hung down on the side over the walls forming a shelter. The fabric used to create these curtains—and all of the other fabrics that would be used in the Tabernacle—was dyed with four colors:

- *Argaman*: maroon—resembling soil/earth
- *Techeiles*: turquoise—resembling water
- *Shesh v'izzim*: off-white linen/bleached goat's hair—resembling wind
- *Tolaas shani*: red—resembling fire

The Tabernacle itself consisted of three main sections and a "hidden" fourth.

1. A courtyard where sacrifices were consumed on an Altar.
2. A sanctuary with the Incense Altar, Menorah, and a Table where the showbread rested.
3. The Holy of Holies where the famous Ark held the tablets.

Resting on top of the ark in the Holy of Holies were the Cherubs, images of two young children with wings. It is here where the energy of prophecy would descend into the world. This was considered a domain of its own.

These four sections, the various vessels that could be found in them, and the services that would be performed in them, reflected the inner world of man and the tools necessary to elevate the four inner elements. The connection is as follows:

INNER REALM	MISHKAN	VESSELS
Physicality (Earth)	Courtyard	Earthen Altar
Emotions (Water)	Sanctuary	Water basin, *Menorah*, Table, Incense Altar
Thoughts (Wind)	Holy of Holies	Ark of the Covenant
Will (Fire)	Cherubim	The empty space in between the Cherubs where prophecy descended

Let's explore these sections in greater detail.

THE COURTYARD AND THE EARTH ELEMENT

The Courtyard's main vessel was the Altar, where animal offerings and other offerings would be brought daily. The Altar must stand upon earth and is referred to as the "earthen Altar." According to our sages, the body of Adam, the first man, was created from earth taken from this spot.

The service of bringing sacrifices connects very much to the elevation of the earth element. Earth is the element of physicality, which is considered the most base and "animalistic" part of us. Bringing an animal as an offering is symbolic of elevating the most base and animistic part of ourselves. We saw how the corruption of the earth element happens through sluggishness. In contradistinction to that, a main aspect of bringing these offerings was that they required the trait of enthusiasm and alacrity.[1] To affect this sort of transformation from mundane to holy would require excitement and energy, as is true in our lives as well.

ALL ROUTINES ARE IMPORTANT, BUT PERHAPS THE MOST IMPORTANT OF THEM ALL IS ONE'S MORNING ROUTINE, WHICH STARTS THE DAY OFF ON EITHER AN ENERGETIC LEG OR A LAZY ONE.

The elevation of the earth element requires a person to stay consistent and committed to routine and resolutions, no matter whether he is in the mood or not. All routines are important, but perhaps the most important of them all is one's morning routine, which starts the day off on either an energetic leg or a lazy one. The sacrifice services in the Tabernacle began each day with a sacrifice called the *Korban Tamid*, which literally means the "consistent animal offering." The daily routine ended with this same offering. All other Temple services would happen in between these two. The message was that in order to thrive and elevate this earthly part of ourselves, one needs to be committed to a consistent routine—especially to start the day and to end it.

---

1 See *Rashi*, Leviticus 6:2.

THE SANCTUARY AND THE WATER ELEMENT

Before entering the Sanctuary, one would encounter the *Kiyor*, a large copper basin that held water, from which the Kohanim, the priests, would wash their hands and feet before doing the Temple service.

The copper from which the *Kiyor* was made had a unique origin that connects us back to the essence of the water element. Our Sages teach that it was made out of copper mirrors. When the Jewish People were donating materials for the building of the Tabernacle, the women came to donate the copper mirrors that they had used to beautify themselves back in Egypt.

We saw earlier, in chapter five, how it was with these mirrors that the women brought intimate life back to their marriage, emotional life back to their husbands, and new life into the world by conceiving Jewish children. When their husbands would be exhausted in the fields, the women would go out and greet them and give them food and drink. They would then playfully entice them by holding the mirror up to both of them and teasing them by saying, "I am more attractive than you." Using this tactic, she would awaken his desire leading to the proliferation of the Jewish nation. At first, Moses was uncomfortable accepting these mirrors for something so holy as the Tabernacle, until God told Moses to accept them, "for they are most precious to Me of all."

As we move deeper into the Sanctuary, we find a golden *Menorah*, whose lamps would be lit each evening, and a golden Table upon which twelves loaves of bread would rest upon shelves. Miraculously, the bread would remain there from Shabbat to Shabbat and remain fresh. Here, too, we find deep symbolisms to love and peace in the home, and, specifically, to the women's role in that.

Our Sages teach that there are three mitzvos that are specifically reserved for the Jewish woman:

- The first is immersing in a mikvah in order to become ritually pure.
- The second is lighting Shabbat candles.
- The third is the separating of *challah*, performed by removing a piece of the dough when she is baking bread.

All of these rituals are auspicious for bringing spiritual blessing into the home and increasing the love and the peace of the various members of the household. The vessels of the Sanctuary and these rituals parallel one another:

- The water basin as well as the mikvah are both symbols of purity.
- The *Menorah* and the Shabbat candles both bring light to their respective environments.
- The showbread in the Sanctuary and the fresh Shabbat challah are both symbols of the blessings and abundance that enter into a home filled with holiness.

Hence, we see a direct correlation between the vessels of the sanctuary and the peace and intimacy that a women can manifest in her home!

A final vessel that stood in the sanctuary was the Golden Altar. This Altar was not meant for animal sacrifices, but, rather, for an incense offering called the *Ketores*. In the Torah, incense is always connected to emotions, as in the verse "oil and incense gladden the heart."[2] The word for "incense," *ketores*, reflects the Aramaic word *kitra*, or the Hebrew word *kesher*, a knot or connection. This too reflected the deep feelings of connection to others and to God that one yearns to feel within the inner realm of one's emotions.

THE HOLY OF HOLIES AND THE WIND ELEMENT

THE ARK TEACHES US OF THE NECESSITY TO SANCTIFY OUR THOUGHTS BY CONTROLLING OUR EYES AND EARS AND THE STIMULI THAT WE ALLOW TO ENTER INTO OUR MIND.

Separating the Sanctuary from the Holy of Holies was a curtain called the *Paroches*, made of various materials and containing images of winged angels on them. The commentaries observe that the Torah's instruction, "the curtain shall serve you as a partition between the Holy and the Holy of Holies,"[3] mirrors another verse in the beginning of the Torah. On Day Two of the Creation narrative, God creates the sky using the words, "Let there be a partition in the midst of the water, that it may

2 Proverbs 27:9.

3 Exodus 26:33.

separate water from water."[4] We therefore see how before entering into the Holy of Holies, we are meant to encounter a representation of the sky, and therefore the wind element. The winged images on the curtain may further be linked to this visual.

Once inside, one would encounter the Ark of the Covenant, a three-layered box containing, amongst other things, the two tablets that were given at Sinai. As this section is meant to represent the intellect, the features of the Ark were meant to resemble the human brain:[5]

- The three boxes are meant to symbolize the three membranes that surround the brain.
- The two tablets parallel the two hemispheres of the brain.
- The Ark would be carried by two poles on each side, connected to the Ark through two rings each. This parallels the powers of vision and hearing, the intellect's main two modes of intake, with the two rings representing the two eyes and the two ears.

The Ark teaches us of the necessity to sanctify our thoughts by controlling our eyes and ears and the stimuli that we allow to enter into our mind. The holy tablets inside the Ark were a reminder that our minds should be filled with those holy thoughts.

THE CHERUBS AND THE FIRE ELEMENT

The cherubs, the two-winged figures that stood upon the Ark, are connected to the element of fire. The angels themselves that are closest to God are referred to as *seraphim*, fiery angels. The spirit of prophecy would enter into the physical realm in the space between these cherubs. As we have seen previously, prophecy is associated with the element of fire. God first spoke to Moses from a burning bush, and the Jewish People received the Torah on a burning mountain. As we let go of our own physical attachment and become in tune with the true essence of ourselves, we feel ourselves expanding and getting in touch with this highest level of our consciousness. As our Sages teach, if we are not prophets ourselves, we are certainly the children of prophets!

---

4 Genesis 1:6.

5 See *Malbim, Parashas Terumah*, in his essay entitled "*Rimzei HaMishkan.*"

With this new framework of how to view the Tabernacle, we now understand why the Torah goes into such detail, and why this is the grand finale of the book of the Exodus. The Tabernacle is the model of the perfected man. The entire book of Exodus was about achieving inner freedom and raising ourselves up from the entrapment of our inner Mitzrayim. After taking us on the journey from enslavement to freedom, and showing us how to RULE over the four inner elements, the Torah now shows us the model of the liberated man through the construction of the Tabernacle. As we study it, we look back in our own mirrors and ask ourselves whether we are reaching the full heights of our potential, and whether we are building a sanctuary inside of ourselves.

THE TABERNACLE GIVES US A VISUAL THAT WE CAN HOLD IN OUR MINDS THROUGHOUT THE DAY.

The Tabernacle gives us a visual that we can hold in our minds throughout the day. When we start our day in the morning, we can visualize how we are standing in the courtyard of the Tabernacle, ready to perform our holy service with enthusiasm and energy, doing the important things first.

When we infuse our day with holy emotion, elevate the mundane aspects to holiness, we are turning our world into a sanctuary for holiness. When we engage in Torah study and the pursuit of truth, we are turning our mind into a holy of holies. And we try to awaken our highest selves by taking time throughout the day to detach from the material world and try to move beyond our ego, we are like the cherubs that are reaching up to heaven, trying to access the highest heights of spiritual consciousness.

Just like the Tabernacle, which accompanied the Jewish People throughout their forty-year sojourn in the desert, adding holiness and connection to the most desolate of places, we have the ability to become conduits for the Divine Presence to rest wherever we find ourselves throughout our day. Just like the Tabernacle, we ourselves are portable sanctuaries. As we go through the various stops in our own life, we are able to transform even the most mundane activities into infinite moments of spiritual connection.

summary

- The Tabernacle is the grand finale and a central focus of the book of the Exodus because it was modeled after the perfected human being. It was not simply a house for God to dwell in, but a conduit for God to rest upon every single Jew.
- The four sections of the Tabernacle—the Courtyard, the Sanctuary, the Holy of Holies, and the Cherubs—and the vessels that are in each of them, each connect to one of the four inner elements and symbolize what perfection in that area would look like.
- As we move through our day, we should envision that we are a walking Tabernacle and that we are trying to build a sanctuary inside of us. When we work to perfect the four inner elements, we are transforming ourselves into a Temple for the Divine Presence to rest.

chapter eighteen

THE FIFTH CUP

THE CUP OF ELIJAH

Each year, at the Passover Seder, we get together to celebrate our freedom. We drink the four cups of wine to commemorate the four terms of redemption:

- *Ve'hotzeisi*—I will take you out from under the burdens of Egypt.
- *Ve'hitzalti*—I will save you from their servitude.
- *Ve'gaalti*—I will redeem you with an outstretched arm.
- *Ve'lakachti*—I will take you to be My people.

We have seen how the four terms of redemption parallel the four elements of our inner world and how each stage of the redemption was exploding with lessons about our own personal journey toward inner freedom and how to RULE over the *yetzer hara*, the negative internal voice that tries to take control of this inner kingdom.

But everybody knows that four cups do not tell the entire story. As the Seder moves into its final phase, after the meal is over and the afikoman eaten, we pour a special cup of wine known as the "Cup of Elijah." The wine poured into this cup remains untouched for the rest of the Seder.

What is the purpose of this cup? What is its message? Why does it belong to the prophet-turned-angel Elijah, when none of the other cups seem to have an owner?

And does it ruin our presentation of how the cups align perfectly with the four terms of redemption and the four inner elements? Does this cup carry a message for us in context of our discussion that we can make relevant to our own journey toward inner freedom?

Not only does this fifth cup not ruin our presentation, but on the contrary—it seems to call our attention to a hidden number five that is consistent throughout. If we look back at the verses where God is sharing the four terms of redemption, the very next verse seems to allude to yet a fifth term:

> *I will bring you into the land that I swore to give to Abraham, Isaac, and Jacob, and I will give it to you for possession.*[1]

This final promise seems to fit together perfectly with the previous four, making us wonder why indeed we don't call it the five terms of redemption. But this fifth one is different. The Seder is a tradition that has carried the Jewish People for thousands of years, the bulk of which were celebrated outside of Israel. Throughout the ages, Jews have gone their entire life without ever being able to lay their eyes on Israel or with any hope that their children would. For them, Israel was a pipe dream.

A core belief in Judaism is that the world is on a constant journey toward a time in the future when all the pain of the world will cease, all war will end, and all the brokenness will be repaired. These days were spoken about throughout the Torah, the prophets, our Sages, and great rabbis throughout history.

It is referred to as the days of the Messiah, or Mashiach, highlighted by the ingathering of the Jewish People from exile, a return to the land of Israel, universal recognition of the oneness of God, and the rebuilding of the Holy Temple with its prominence as a world center for spirituality. It is one of the fundamental tenets of Jewish belief, and it is woven into almost all of the prayer services. This promising vision has made such an imprint on human belief that many religions and spiritual traditions have some form of this dream as part of their tradition.

As each generation takes the stage, new movements, new advances, and new technologies are paving the way for this new world. As the time gets closer, new painful challenges arise that inevitably propel us forward. They are like the birth pangs of a woman in labor, with each

---

1 Exodus 6:8.

contraction bringing the baby one step closer to taking his first breath. The mother knows that at any moment, that next strong contraction might be the one that will push the baby to the point of emerging in the light of the world. In our world, too, all of the pain is just part of the process, pushing us closer to the birth of the Mashiach.

Jewish tradition teaches that the prophet Elijah will appear in order to herald the coming of Mashiach. This is based on the words of the prophet, "Behold, I will send to you Elijah the Prophet before the arrival of the great and awesome day of God."

The fifth cup is referred to as the cup of Elijah because it symbolizes a time that we are yearning for, i.e., the permanent realization of the fifth term of redemption, "I will bring you into the land which I swore to give to Abraham, Isaac, and Jacob," though it may not be tangible for us yet.

HIGH FIVE

The Torah itself indicates the elusive nature of the fifth level of redemption. After five books building up to the fulfillment of God's promise to Abraham that his children would enter into Israel, and after forty years of wandering in the desert in order to prepare themselves for their inheritance, the Torah abruptly ends without telling us of their deliverance. It is only in the book of Joshua, the opening book of the section of the Torah called "Prophets," which is of lower status than the actual Five Books of Moses, that we learn about the Jewish People's actual entry into the land. One would think that this should be the happy ending, the grand finale of the Five Books of Moses. Yet, the Torah leaves us with a cliffhanger.

THE TORAH WANTS TO KEEP US YEARNING, KNOWING THAT THERE IS SOMETHING MORE, SOMETHING THAT WE HAVE YET TO ACHIEVE.

Clearly, the Torah does not want to leave us with a feeling of satisfaction of having arrived. Clearly, the Torah wants to keep us yearning, knowing that there is something more, something that we have yet to achieve.

The thirst that we feel at the end of the Torah is the thirst that exiled Jews throughout the ages would feel. Most of Jewish history would be a story of yearning and hoping and praying for that final redemption. It seems that God's master plan for us was to be a nation of travelers and sojourners, never getting too comfortable with the status quo.

Our Seder night may be a celebration of the Exodus and the freedom that we achieved on that night, but it is also a story about a long exile from which we are hoping to be liberated. We recreate a night that we were still in Egypt, knowing that at any moment we would have to pack our bags and go. This is meant to remind us to not get too comfortable, because this is just a stop on a much bigger journey. The Seder is at night, a time of darkness, a time that symbolizes exile, but is meant to extend until the morning, symbolizing redemption.

Though we have been in exile for thousands of years, our Sages frame it as four exiles: Babylon (who destroyed the First Temple), Persia (where the Purim story occurred), Greece (who persecuted us during the Chanukah story) and Rome (who destroyed the Second Temple). Therefore, four is the number that represents exile. Five is the number that represents redemption.

In the early chapters of this book, we introduced the four inner realms of earth, water, wind, and fire as levels of our lower soul. We mentioned that there is actually a fifth element, a Godly soul. We saw throughout the chapters of this book that the four realms of the lower soul are places of turmoil and struggle. We strive to elevate them, but they are vulnerable to the entrapments of the *yetzer hara*, the force of negativity.

The fifth dimension, the Godly soul, is untouchable and pure, but it is concealed. We feel its influence inside of us all the time in the form of inspiration and ecstasy. Then, just as quickly, it is gone. So, we yearn for it and we pray for it a little more. And when it returns to us, we feel it, yet a bit stronger for a bit longer. And then the cycle repeats itself.

The four cups of wine, like the four terms of redemption and the four inner elements, are all about the struggle, because that is why we exist: to fight the Pharaohs, to fight the Amalekites, to fight the snakes of the Garden of Eden, and to refine the jewel that is inside of us. The fifth cup, like the fifth term of redemption and the fifth element, is about what we are looking toward and yearning for. But *in this lifetime, every destination is just the beginning of a new journey*.

Each year, we sit down at the Seder and read the words of the Haggadah that instruct us to see ourselves as if we left Egypt. It is certainly a daunting task to put ourselves in the shoes of our ancestors of three thousand years ago.

Through the lens of the four elements, we are able to unpack the deeper messages of the story of the enslavement in Egypt and the story of the Exodus to show that the Torah is really trying to guide us along in our own journey toward inner freedom.

The struggles of humanity will always boil down to the very same roots. Times change, but the struggles remain the same. Humanity is on a journey to elevate the four elements and discover the hidden fifth, and we are all pieces of that puzzle as we encounter those challenges in our day-to-day life.

As we drink the four cups of wine and set our eyes on the fifth cup, let us rejoice in our successes and in the knowledge that even though we fall often and fall hard, we have a loving parent in heaven and in our hearts who is cheering for us and holding our hand throughout the journey.

We just need to take that next step!

Next year in Jerusalem!

summary

- In addition to the four cups that correspond to the four promises of redemption, there is also a fifth cup, the cup of Elijah, which corresponds to God's promise to bring the Jewish People into the land of Israel.
- Elijah is the personality who is referred to by the prophets as the one who is going to usher in the final redemption, our ultimate return back to the Holy Land to rebuild the Temple as a world center for spirituality.
- The fifth cup, like the fifth element, reminds us that there is always the next phase, there is always something more that may be hidden today, but if we continue our climb upward, will be revealed to us at just the right time.

EPILOGUE

IN 2021, as part of the launch of my first book, I had the opportunity to teach a series of classes to a group of men and women who had each gone through a very long and intense journey of addiction recovery. The group consisted of some of the most incredible people whom I have ever been privileged to meet: successful in their professions and deeply aware of their souls and their purpose. The classes took place during the weeks leading up to the holiday of Passover, and the goal of the talks was to speak about the connection between the Passover story and overcoming our own inner struggles.

I shared with them some of the ideas of this book and how the four elements are connected to the various stages of our journey from being in a place of stuck-ness to feeling fully free.

In the days following, I received an email from one of the attendees of the class.

> *I started using drugs when I was thirteen. Didn't stop until I was fifty-six. I used longer than the Jews wandering in Sinai! I am grateful for the life I have today and what I can still learn because I am willing. I have found so many parallels to recovery in the Torah.*
>
> *I can so totally relate to what you taught us. My very early recovery was definitely Earth, I was just copying others and going through the motions because that's all I was capable of. I progressed to Water and became inquisitive, but still had no real idea of what I was searching for. Years later, I entered the Wind phase, and started getting real clarity of what I wanted and who I wanted to be. Finally, I found Fire and realized Hashem is my Higher Power.*

> *Today, I know that I am right where I should be. I am so grateful to be so loved by Hashem. I am so grateful.*

When Moses stood at the burning bush, before the wheels of redemption had been set in motion, he asks God to reveal to him the Divine name that he should relate to the Jewish People. God tells Moses to tell the Jewish People that He is called "*Ehe-yeh asher Ehe-yeh*" meaning, "I will be who I will be," Our Sages interpret this message as, "I am with you now in this struggle, and I will be with you in future struggles."

We are that future.

No matter where a person finds himself, no matter how badly one feels that he has fallen and feels distant from God, those words are meant to reassure a person: "I am with you in this, too. Turn to Me and you will find Me even here in whatever dark Mitzrayim that you are going through."

The word *Ehe-yeh* has the numerical value of twenty-one (*aleph*=1, *hei*=5, *yud*=10, *hei*=5). God's name is this word *Ehe-yeh*, repeated twice, equaling forty-two. The Jewish People would make forty-two stops in the desert en route to the land of Israel. They are symbolic of the various stops that we make throughout our life, the different steps necessary to accomplish our mission in this world.

God was communicating a message that would echo throughout history, down to you and me, in every one of the stops that we make in our own wanderings.

> *I will be with you every step of the way. It will look and feel different every time. Sometimes, it will be a high and sometimes it will be a low. But pay attention because every step of the way will be another revelation for those who are open to see it.*

As dark and as difficult as things seem from time to time, in truth, the seeds of redemption are taking root, waiting to shoot forth an even higher version of ourselves. So, we give one push forward to try to break through the dirt, and then another and then another. With each push, we discover something new about God and about ourselves. And then, sooner than we can even anticipate, the breakthrough comes and we find our way en route to the Promised Land! Seas begin to split for us, and the evil forces that try and stop us are washed away. The things that we need for our growth seem to rain down from heaven in ways that can only be explained as supernatural. And we discover our unique missions in this world. Our inner fire. Our crown.

And just as we feel that we have made it, that we have conquered, we come to the beautiful realization that...our journey has only just begun.

GLOSSARY

Bereishis: lit. in the beginning; the Hebrew title of the first book of the Torah, also known as the Book of Genesis.

bittul ha'yesh: nullification of the ego, ego dissolution.

chochmah: wisdom; specifically, information that can be learned and received.

daas: lit. knowledge; often implies a deep experiential knowledge of something and sometimes refers to higher consciousness.

deveikus: connection; cleaving.

emes: truth.

emunah: faith, belief.

gematria: the study of numerology.

gevurah: strength, discipline.

Haggadah: Ancient text that is read at the Passover seder.

Kabbalah: Jewish mysticism and the study of the secrets of the Torah.

kavod: honor.

kiddush: blessing that is recited to greet and sanctify Shabbat and festivals.

Mah Nishtanah: lit. "what is different?"; the title of the section of the Passover seder when the four questions are recited.

matzoh: unleavened bread.

middos: lit. measurements; used to refer to human attributes and character traits.

Midrash: lit. exposition. The texts known as Midrash are a collection of early Jewish interpretations of and commentary on the Torah, as taught by the same rabbis who are featured in the Mishnah.

Mishkan: Tabernacle; the portable Temple that accompanied the Israelites in the desert.

Mitzrayim (meitzar): the Torah's name for Egypt. The root *meitzar* means constriction or a narrow place.

mitzvah (pl.–mitzvos): one of the 613 commandments or good deeds related to them.

mikvah: pool of natural water used for ritual immersion.

modeh: thank, praise, admit.

nefesh: life force or spirit; the lowest level of the five soul levels.

neshamah: breath of life; the middle level of the five soul levels.

Seder: lit. order; refers to the Passover evening ceremony and the many traditions that are performed.

Shechinah: the Divine Presence that, according to Kabbalah, dwells in the physical world.

Shemos: lit. names; the Hebrew title of the second book of the Torah, also known as the Book of Exodus.

Talmud: largest and most widely studied compilation of Jewish writings in numerous volumes, in which Jewish law and thought is discussed and debated.

tikkun: repairing of damage.

yetzer hara: impulse or inclination for either bad or to fill one's physical desires.

yetzer tov: impulse or inclination for good and for spirituality.

zerizus: alacrity, quickness.

AUTHORS AND WORKS CITED

Alshich Hakadosh: Rabbi Moshe Alshich (1508–93) was a prominent rabbi and Biblical commentator in the holy of city of Safed. His brilliant lectures on the Torah, which were recorded and printed, begin with a series of questions on a segment of Torah, which he answers using great depth, often drawing from some of the more esoteric wisdom of our sages.

Arizal: Rabbi Isaac Luria (1534–72), known as Ari (meaning "The Lion"), or "*Arizal*" (the Ari of blessed memory), was a leading rabbi and Kabbalist in the holy city of Safed. Considered the father of contemporary Kabbalah, he gave a new language and presentation to ancient Kabbalistic ideas.

Baal Shem Tov: Rabbi Yisroel ben Eliezer (1700–60), known as the Baal Shem Tov (Master of the Good Name), was a Kabbalist and healer who lived in the Ukraine. He is the founder of the Chassidic movement, and his disciples founded the great Chassidic dynasties.

Ethics of our Fathers: *Pirkei Avos*, lit. "Chapters of Our Fathers," is a section of the Mishnah, one of the most fundamental works of the Jewish Oral Law, authored in the third-century CE. While most of the books of Mishnah focus on Jewish law, *Pirkei Avos* is devoted exclusively to the ethical and moral statements of the Sages.

Maimonides: Rabbi Moshe Ben Maimon (1135–1204), known by the acronym *Rambam*, was a Rabbinic authority, philosopher, and doctor in Spain and Egypt. His works, including a codification of the legal content of the Talmud, books on Torah law and Jewish philosophy, and commentary on the classical texts, have been widely studied through the ages.

Malbim: Rabbi Meir Leibush Wisser (1809–79) was a rabbi, Torah commentator, and master of Hebrew grammar. *Malbim* served as rabbi in Poland, Germany, and Romania. He was a fiery defender of Orthodox tradition, and was even imprisoned for it.

Midrash: lit. exposition. The texts known as Midrash are a collection of early Jewish interpretations of and commentary on the Torah, as taught by the same rabbis who are featured in the Mishnah.

Book of Proverbs: a book in the third section (called *Ketuvim*) of the Hebrew Bible exploring values, morals, and the meaning of life. The Hebrew title is *Mishlei Shlomo*, or *The Proverbs of Solomon*, a reference to King Solomon, who, according to Jewish tradition, is its author.

Rabbi Chayim Vital (1543–1620): a rabbi in Safed and the foremost disciple of Isaac Luria (the *Arizal*, see above). He is renowned as the scribe and editor of the *Arizal*'s teachings, as well as a Kabbalist and writer in his own right. He also studied under Rabbi Moshe Alshich and Rabbi Moshe Cordovero. His work, *Shaarei Kedushah*, which is a manual of proper character for aspiring mystics, is quoted in this book and is often quoted regarding the four elements and human character.

Rabbi Dov Ber Maggid of Mezeritch (d. 1772): Primary student of the Baal Shem Tov (see above). Known as the first systematic exponent of the mystical philosophy underlying the Baal Shem Tov's Chassidic movement. His students spread Chassidus throughout Europe, including Elimelech of Lizensk, Shneur Zalman of Liadi, and Menachem Nachum of Chernobyl (see below).

Rabbi Klonymos Kalman Shapiro (1889–1943): Rabbi of Piaseczno, Poland, who authored a number of works and was murdered by the Nazis during the Holocaust. Among his many works, the most well-known is the *Aish Kodesh* (The Holy Fire), which he authored while leading the community in the Warsaw Ghetto.

Rabbi Menachem Nachum Twerski of Chernobyl (1730–98): student of the Baal Shem Tov and the Maggid of Mezeritch, and the author of the work *Meor Einayim*. He was known as a *maggid*, a preacher who seeks to inspire the masses with teachings about ethics, spirituality, and religious observance.

Rabbi Mordechai Yosef Leiner of Izhbitz (1801–54): was a brilliant and often controversial Chassidic thinker and founder of the Izhbitza-Radzyn dynasty. He is best known for his work *Mei Hashiloach*, a collection of his teachings on the weekly Torah portion and Jewish holidays.

Rabbi Moshe Chaim Luzzatto (1707–46): Often referred to as the *Ramchal*, he was a prominent Italian Jewish rabbi, Kabbalist, and philosopher. He authored many works on ethics, philosophy and Kabbalah. His works *Mesilas Yesharim* (Path of the Just) and *Derech Hashem* (The Way of God) are quoted throughout this book.

Rabbi Nachman of Breslov (1772–1810): The great-grandson of the Baal Shem Tov, Rabbi Nachman was a Chassidic leader and founder of the Breslov Chassidic movement. He placed great emphasis on joy, happiness, and hope, as well as meditating and having conversations with God while alone in nature. Today, many travel to his grave in Uman, Ukraine, to pray, especially on Rosh Hashanah.

Rabbi Natan Sternhartz of Breslov (1780–1844): the chief disciple and scribe of Rabbi Nachman of Breslov. He wrote down the teachings of Rabbi Nachman and is credited with promoting and expanding the Breslov movement after Rabbi Nachman's death.

Rabbi Shlomo Yitzchaki (1040–1104): Known by the acronym *Rashi*, a medieval French rabbi who was the leading commentator on the Bible and Talmud, providing a running commentary that is clear and concise, focusing on the simple interpretation.

Rabbi Tzadok HaKohen Rabinowitz (1823–1900): Famed master of Chassidic thought and prolific author in all areas of Judaism, including law, Chassidus, Kabbalah, and ethics. He also wrote scholarly essays on astronomy, geometry, and algebra. He became part of the Chassidic movement as an adult, and refused to hold any Rabbinic position until late in his life.

Sefas Emes: Rabbi Yehudah Aryeh Leib Alter (1847–1905) was a Chassidic rabbi and one of the greatest Torah scholars of his generation. Under his leadership, the Gerrer dynasty became the largest Chassidic group in Poland. His works, which were published posthumously, are all entitled *Sefas Emes* and deal with the weekly Torah portion, the Talmud, and on the Code of Jewish law.

Zohar: The mystical commentary on the Torah that is widely considered the foundational work of Kabbalah. The *Zohar* was first publicized by Moses de León in the thirteenth century, but it is attributed to the recorded teachings of Rabbi Shimon bar Yochai by his students in the second century.

ABOUT THE AUTHOR

RABBI SHLOMO BUXBAUM is a passionate Jewish educator, motivational speaker, and life coach in the Greater Washington, D.C., area, working with both families and young adults from all different Jewish backgrounds. A student of Yeshivas Toras Moshe and the Mirrer Yeshiva, Rabbi Buxbaum received rabbinic ordination from Aish HaTorah and Rabbi Zalman Nechemia Goldberg, *zt"l*. Rabbi Buxbaum was the rabbi of Aish HaTorah of Greater Washington for eight years before launching the Lev Experience together with his wife, Devorah, with the mission of empowering individuals to find greater meaning, purpose, and possibilities in life by deepening their connection to Jewish wisdom and values. Rabbi Buxbaum also hosts a weekly podcast called "The Empowered Jewish Living Podcast," lectures for various other educational institutions in Maryland, and is a frequent scholar-in-residence throughout America. Rabbi Buxbaum, his wife, and their six children live in Silver Spring, Maryland.